What To Do
When Faith
Seems Weak
& Victory Lost

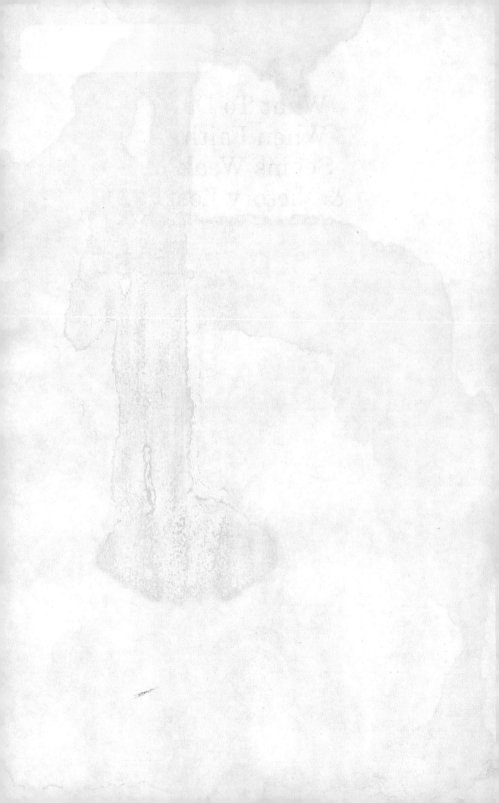

What To Do When Faith Seems Weak & Victory Lost

Kenneth E. Hagin

Unless otherwise indicated, all Scripture quotations in this volume are from the *King James Version* of the Bible.

Eighteenth Printing 2002

ISBN 0-89276-501-1

In the U.S. write:
Kenneth Hagin Ministries
P.O. Box 50126
Tulsa, OK 74150-0126
1-888-28-FAITH
www.rhema.org

In Canada write:
Kenneth Hagin Ministries
P.O. Box 335, Station D,
Etobicoke (Toronto), Ontario
Canada, M9A 4X3

Contents

1. Recognizing the Source 11

2. Be Sure the Promises of God Cover the Things You Ask For 25

3. Be Sure You Are Not Living in Sin 37

4. Be Sure No Doubt or Unbelief Is Permitted in Your Life 53

5. Sincerely Desire the Benefit 75

6. Ask God in Faith Nothing Wavering 89

7. Do Not Tolerate a Thought to the Contrary 95

8. Count the Thing Done 99

9. Give Glory to God 111

10. Act as Though You Have Received 115

In Summation 117

Preface

I have begun this book with two scriptures (2 Cor. 4:4 and Eph. 6:10-17) which tell us that our enemy is Satan.

But God has given us the equipment for victory over Satan! There is no need for us to be overcome by him. (If we are overcome, it is our fault, not God's.) There is no need for us to be defeated. (If we are defeated, it is our fault, not God's.) God has given us His Word. God's Word and God's armor are all the equipment we need to enforce the defeat of Satan and his forces.

Yet I meet Christians all the time who have problems. They have come to the place where they say, "I don't know what to do." (Have you ever been there?) That's the reason I wrote this book. The ten steps outlined in this book, when taken in sequence, will bring you out of defeat and into certain victory!

I am indebted to Rev. Finis Jennings Dake for these ten steps, which he listed in Supplement Nine of his well-known book, *God's Plan for Man*.

Kenneth E. Hagin

"In whom the god of this world hath blinded the minds of them which believe not, lest the light of the glorious gospel of Christ, who is the image of God, should shine unto them."

—2 Corinthians 4:4

"Finally, my brethren, be strong in the Lord, and in the power of his might.
Put on the whole armour of God, that ye may be able to stand against the wiles of the devil.
For we wrestle not against flesh and blood, but against principalities, against powers, against the rulers of the darkness of this world, against spiritual wickedness in high places.
Wherefore take unto you the whole armour of God, that ye may be able to withstand in the evil day, and having done all to stand.
Stand therefore, having your loins girt about with truth, and having on the breastplate of righteousness;
And your feet shod with the preparation of the gospel of peace;
Above all, taking the shield of faith, wherewith ye shall be able to quench all the fiery darts of the wicked.
And take the helmet of salvation, and the sword of the Spirit, which is the word of God."

—Ephesians 6:10-17

Step One: Recognize the source of the opposition as being Satan—and stand your ground!

So many times people do not know whether God or the devil is doing certain things. "Well," they say, "maybe the Lord is trying to teach me something."

I remember hearing an evangelist years ago. He'd had a tent which seated 20,000 people. But when he put it up down in Texas, one of those Texas tornadoes came along and blew it away. At this meeting they were taking up a special offering to help him get another tent. I remember he said, and I almost fell off the bench when I heard him say it, "I don't know whether God or the devil blew away my tent."

God is not out blowing down gospel tents! God is out putting them up!

"Yes," somebody said, "but God allowed it."

God is not the god of this world. Second Corinthians 4:4 calls Satan the god of this world. And the laws governing

11

the earth today very largely came into being with the fall of man and the curse upon the earth.

It is because people do not understand this that they accuse God of accidents, of sickness, of the death of loved ones, of storms, catastrophes, earthquakes, and floods. God is not responsible for, nor the author of, any one of those things.

Jesus set aside these natural laws, as we understand them, in order to bless humanity. Jesus stood on board that ship and rebuked that storm, saying, "Peace, be still." According to John 14:10 it was God in Him who did that work. If God caused the storm, God would be working against Himself in causing it to cease.

It was the same with the healings Jesus performed. Jesus said, "The Father in me, He doeth the works." All the healings, all the miracles, all the works that Jesus did, God did. If God were the author of sickness and disease, and God healed people through Jesus, then God worked against Himself.

That cannot be. For Jesus said, " . . . *if a kingdom be divided against itself, that kingdom cannot stand. And if a house be divided against itself, that house cannot stand"* (Mark 3:24,25).

Determine the Source

It is very easy to find out where things come from. The Lord Jesus Christ Himself contrasted His works with the works of the devil in John 10:10.

> **JOHN 10:10**
> 10 The thief cometh not, but for to steal, and to kill,

**and to destroy: I am come that they might have life,
and that they might have it more abundantly.**

In contrasting His works with the works of the devil,
Jesus is contrasting God's works with the works of the
devil. For on one occasion Jesus said, *"I must work the
works of him that sent me while it is day: the night cometh
when no man can work"* (John 9:4). On another occasion
when one disciple said to Him, *"Show us the Father,"* Jesus
answered, *"He that hath seen me hath seen the Father
. . . the Father that dwelleth in me, he doeth the works"*
(John 14:9,10). **If you want to see God at work, look at
Jesus.**

It would absolutely erase all confusion as to where a
thing is coming from if we would listen to the Word of God.

Most of us, however, from the time we were children,
and before we could really read and get into the Word of
God for ourselves, were religiously brainwashed. We have
heard unscriptural things said all our lives—and
sometimes even preached in the church we attended.
What we heard was just the human mind trying to solve
spiritual problems. And the human mind cannot solve
spiritual problems.

If you will get into the Word of God, it will straighten
out your thinking. Think in line with what God's Word
says—not necessarily with what you have been taught it
says, nor what somebody told you it says. Ask yourself,
"What does the Word of God say?"

Let's examine what Jesus said in contrasting His
works with the works of the devil.

Jesus said, *"The thief. . . . "* He's not calling God a
thief. God is not a thief. Jesus is not a thief. The devil is.
Jesus calls the devil a thief.

Jesus said, *"The thief cometh not, but for to steal, and to kill, and to destroy . . . . "* That which steals, that which kills, that which destroys is a thief. All such is the devil's work—not God's.

You need to realize this: Many times, particularly in the Old Testament, when it talks about God's doing something, He did not actually perform it. In other words, He was not the *agent* who did it. He did not send evil on anyone. God already had warned them, "If you sin, these things will happen to you."

Suppose, for instance, a man climbs up on the house, then falls off and breaks his leg. God put into motion the law of gravity. But the man could not say, "God broke my leg," or, "God pushed me off the roof," or even, "God did it." No. God put into motion the law of gravity; the man violated it, and reaped the results.

It is true that God is the author of the law of gravity. But He did not intend for the man to break his leg. He did not intend for him to fall. The man fell off accidentally, or because he was careless.

Now then, when certain things happen in life—such as sickness and disease, catastrophe, etc.—and people say, "God did it," no, He did not. They happen because man sinned. Not the individual involved, necessarily, but Adam sinned—and all mankind fell heir to the terrible results. As John Alexander Dowie said, "Sickness is the foul offspring of its mother Sin and its father Satan."

We all have sinned and come short of the glory of God (Rom. 3:23). But God did not intend that we would sin. God warned man these things would happen. But He did not intend they would happen. They happened because man listened to the devil.

Satan was not originally the god of this world; Adam was. Go back to the Book of Beginnings, the Book of Genesis. God made the world and the fullness thereof—and it was all good. There was not anything that was bad. Then He made His man Adam and He said, "Adam, I give you dominion over all the work of my hands." (That's over the earth and everything.) "You dominate." Or, in other words, "I am making you god of this world. You run it."

But Adam committed high treason and sold out to the devil. He did not have the moral right to do it, but he did have the legal right. Then the devil began to dominate upon the earth. He became the god of this world (2 Cor. 4:4).

The Bible record of the temptation of Jesus sheds light we need to see about Satan's domination upon the earth.

> **LUKE 4:5-8**
> 5 And the devil, taking him (Jesus) up into an high mountain, shewed unto him all the kingdoms of the world in a moment of time.
> 6 And the devil said unto him, All this power will I give thee, and the glory of them: FOR THAT IS DELIVERED UNTO ME; And to whomsoever I will I give it.
> 7 If thou therefore wilt worship me, all shall be thine.
> 8 And Jesus answered and said unto him, Get thee behind me, Satan: for it is written, Thou shalt worship the Lord thy God, and him only shalt thou serve.

I heard a radio preacher say, "That didn't belong to Satan. It all belonged to God. Satan just lied."

If that were the case, Jesus would have known it, and there would have been no temptation. The Bible says that Jesus was tempted.

That poor radio preacher unconsciously accused the

Lord Jesus Christ of perpetrating a fraud, becoming partner to a lie, and being dishonest. For if this were not a real temptation, Jesus was dishonest.

Jesus did not dispute for a moment that this was delivered unto Satan (v. 6). Who delivered it to him? Adam did.

The Bible tells us that when Satan is finally eliminated from the earth, there will be nothing which hurts or destroys.

That will be a great day. But, thank God, we do not have to let Satan dominate us now. Even though he is the god of this world, he does not have the right to dominate the Church. He does not have the right to dominate us as believers.

Stand Your Ground

It is important to recognize that the source of the opposition is Satan—and to stand your ground.

Too many people are ready to give up on something instead of recognizing that it is Satan who is trying to keep it from happening. Many of the things we pray about—finances, healing, and so on—have to come to pass in this world realm. And Satan is at work here. He will put up every block he can to keep it from happening. Then if there is the least delay, some people say, "Maybe God doesn't want me to have that after all." They lose out and are defeated when they should have recognized the source of all opposition is Satan and not allowed him to defeat them.

I opened this book with Scripture from the 6th chapter of Ephesians which declares the fact that it is Satan with whom we have to deal. Paul, writing this letter to the

Church, plainly said, *"Finally, my brethren, be strong in the Lord . . . . "* (v. 10).

Somebody said, "Oh, I'm trying to be strong."

It does not say a thing in the world about their being strong. That's where people miss it. They drop back into the natural and try to do it themselves. It does not say anything about the individual's being strong. It says, *"Finally, my brethren, be strong in the Lord . . . . "* It does not say, "Be strong in yourself." It says, *"Be strong in the Lord, and in the power of his might."*

We used to hear people say in testimony meetings, "Pray for me that I will hold out faithful to the end." Bless their hearts, they were just a-workin' and a-strugglin', trying to hold on and hold out. And they didn't know whether they could, or they couldn't.

I use this illustration quite often. On May 11, 1932, a crowd of 10,000 assembled to welcome the world's largest dirigible, the U.S. Navy's $8 million USS *Akron*, to Camp Kearney, San Diego, California. (At that time, the U.S. Government was experimenting with lighter-than-air craft.)

The mooring appeared to be successful. Then a ring that held one of the two mooring cables snapped and the 785-foot airship started to lift. Two groups of sailors holding landing ropes attached to the cables attempted to guide the *Akron* back to its mooring mast, but strong winds buffeted the giant dirigible, and it broke loose, lifting many of the 200 sailors ten to twenty feet off the ground. Some were injured as they fell. Then only three men dangled from the 300-foot cable as the *Akron* continued to ascend.

According to contemporary newspaper accounts,

hysteria prevailed. Women fainted. Officers wept. Enlisted men ran around wildly, unable to help the three desperate men clinging to the cable. Soon, two of the men could hold on no longer, and they plummeted 150 feet and 200 feet to their deaths.

Farther up in the twisted lines, the third sailor, a 19-year-old enlisted man from Oklahoma, braced his feet in some wooden handgrips and quickly lashed other lines attached to the cable around his body. He just kept holding on as the *Akron* rose to 2,000 feet. The horrified onlookers thought that his strength would fail at any moment and he, too, would fall to his death. Half an hour passed. Then the tiny figure moved—the man was alive!

Attempts to lower the giant aircraft were unsuccessful because of the winds. The sailor's two-hour ordeal finally ended when the crew cautiously hauled him inside the airship by hand while the *Akron* circled San Diego.

When people asked him, "How did you hold on so long?" he replied, "I didn't hold on. When I saw I was too far from the ground to let go, I wrapped the ropes around me. I wasn't holding onto them; they were holding me."

While people on the ground were screaming, he was up there enjoying the scenery. He wasn't trusting himself to hold on. He was trusting the rope to hold him. He was swinging free!

That's what God's Word is talking about. *"Be strong in the Lord and in the power of His might."* Just wrap yourself in the promises of God and swing free. Just enjoy yourself. If you try to hold on, you will tire out after a while.

Yes, there is a wily foe against us — but, thank God, we can stand against him.

Somebody said, "I've done all I know to do. What am I to do now?

" . . . having done all, to stand. Stand therefore . . . . " (Eph. 6:13,14). Just keep on standing! That's what you do!

My father left home when I was six. My mother, because of all the problems she'd had with him, had a complete nervous and physical breakdown. So we went to live with our grandparents on her side of the family.

When Granny had to be doing something, such as hanging out the clothes to dry, she would have me watch Momma. Momma had "spells" when she would want to kill herself. I had to watch to see that she didn't get hold of a knife or something dangerous. That made quite an impression on me as a young child.

I'm going to explore a side issue here. My mother was a Christian—but just a baby Christian. She knew Christ as her Savior, but she did not know how to stand, and so on. What if she had killed herself? Would she have been saved? Well, it is possible to be sick in your head just as much as it is possible to be sick in your stomach. Would someone go to hell just because he was sick in his stomach? No. Nor would he go to hell just because he was sick in his head. Being sick in his head would not keep him from going to heaven.

People can be sick in their heads and not even know what they are doing. Momma lived to be 80. Years after she recovered and I was in the ministry, I suddenly began to talk to her one day about having had to watch her and some of those things. "Why, Son, don't you ever say a thing like that," she said. "You know I'm a Christian. I wouldn't have done anything like that. I wouldn't have taken my own life." She had no knowledge of it whatever. I never mentioned it to her again.

Now back to the time when she was having a multitude of problems. Finally she was sent to a Baptist hospital in Dallas and the leading nerve specialist in the southwestern part of the country. After examination, the doctor said that the chances of an operation correcting her blindness were not good. (Because of her mental and physical breakdown, Momma had become blind. Her eyes looked as perfect as anyone's, but due to shock to the nerve of her eye, it was not strong enough for the light.)

"When it comes to nerves," that wise doctor advised her, "you can do more than anybody or any medication you could take. The main thing to do is this—talk to yourself. The Bible says in Ephesians 6:13,14, 'Having done all to stand. Stand therefore.' When you feel these attacks coming on, say to yourself, 'No, I am not going to have an attack.'"

Even we could tell when one of those terrible attacks was coming. She would go into a preliminary attack of depression. She would get to thinking about everything that ever had happened to her in life. You see, her parents had not wanted her to marry my father. Not that he didn't come from a good family—his father was a millionaire. But he was an only son who always had been given everything he wanted. My grandfather spent $50,000— and that was big money then—setting him up in business five different times. But he never made a success of anything. He just ran through the money. When Momma married him against her parents' wishes, she said, "If I make my bed hard, I'll lie on it." She made her bed hard, and she tried to lie on it. But she just could not make it.

If you are not careful, you can get to thinking about the

past—mistakes you made, where you missed it—and get depressed. Then you can get into a spirit of depression. And that opens the door to the devil. You can get so perplexed and depressed and oppressed until you do not know what you are doing, which direction you are going, and hardly what your name is.

We knew nothing about divine healing, praying, and all that, but Momma did heed this doctor's advice. She simply stood her ground. She refused to have any more attacks. A few times she would start to go into one of these periods of depression, but she would do what the doctor said, and never again did she go into one of the violent attacks where her mind was completely gone.

Our preacher did not know how to help her. The doctor knew enough to at least give her Scripture to stand against that thing. The doctor recognized it as an enemy, not a friend. *(The thief is come to steal, to kill, to destroy—I am come that you might have life.)* The doctor instructed her, "Stand against it. Talk to yourself. Say, 'I am not going to have another attack. I am not going to do it.'" She stood her ground. Every symptom left. For more than 50 years thereafter, she never had any nervous problems whatsoever.

That doctor helped Momma see where the opposition was. He helped her understand that she could stand against it. You do not have to yield to things that are wrong. You can stand against them.

Too often though, we limit our idea of what is wrong, or evil, to things like lying, stealing, adultery, murder, etc. All that is evil. All that is wrong. But—there are many other things that are wrong.

The Bible tells us that doubt is evil. It calls the report

those 10 spies brought back after spying out Canaan's Land an "evil report" (Num. 13:32).

I am glad I got hold of these truths when I was just a young man. Since even before I was filled with the Holy Spirit or knew anything about it, this is the practice I always follow if doubt comes. I stop wherever I am—in the middle of a room, the middle of the street, or wherever. If I am alone, I say it aloud. If I am around people, I say it quietly. (You don't want to startle people.) If doubt persists in coming against my mind I say, "Doubt, I resist you." I speak to it. You see, I am recognizing the source of my opposition as the enemy. I am not going to yield to it. It is Satan. "Doubt, I resist you," I say. "In the Name of Jesus I refuse to doubt."

If fear comes—I am tempted to be afraid just as much as anyone else—I speak to it. "Fear," I say, "I resist you."

I recognize fear and doubt as being evil.

If the thought to steal came to me, I would not yield to it. Would you? If you were visiting my house and saw a hundred dollar bill lying on the table, you wouldn't say, "I believe I'll get that. Nobody will see. Brother Hagin left the room." No, you wouldn't yield to it. You would resist it.

You would not get up in church and testify, "I want you to pray for me. The devil is trying to get me to steal a hundred dollars from Brother Hagin." No, you would be ashamed of it.

You would be ashamed to get up and say, "The devil has tempted me to rob a gas station down on the corner. I almost did it. I even pulled in there and stopped. Then I got cold feet. You all pray for me that I won't rob that gas station." No! The very minute such a thought came, you would stand against it. You would recognize its source.

If a thought of doubt comes, if a thought of fear comes, resist it the same way. Speak to it and say, "No, I will not entertain that."

Recognize—if you want to walk in victory—that the source of all opposition is Satan, and stand against it.

Satan is the god of this world. He has a right to be here.

"Brother Hagin," a man said, with a look of real seriousness on his face, "I want you to pray for me."

"What for, Brother?"

Tears came to his eyes. "I want you to pray for me that I won't ever have any more trouble with the devil."

I said, "Do you want me to pray that you will die?"

"No," he said. "I don't want to die."

I said, "The only way in the world you won't have any more trouble with the devil is to die and go on to heaven. As long as you are in this life, you are going to have trouble with him. He is the god of this world."

There is no use in praying that you won't have any more trouble with the devil. He will show up on every corner. He has a right to be here until Adam's lease runs out.

Demons which possessed people would recognize Jesus and cry out to Him, "What have we to do with thee, Jesus, thou Son of God? art thou come hither to torment us before the *time*?" (Matt. 8:29).

The *time* has not yet come. When Adam's lease runs out, then the devil will be a goner. Until then, he has a right to be here.

Blessed be God, we need to realize that we have authority over the devil in the Name of the Lord Jesus Christ. We can stand against him. We can be victorious through the Lord Jesus Christ.

Step Two: Be sure the promises of God—the Scriptures—cover the things you ask for and are believing for.

Faith—Bible Faith—is based on the Word of God. It comes by hearing the Word of God:

ROMANS 10:17
17 So then faith cometh by hearing, and hearing by the word of God.

If you get out beyond the Word of God, you have no basis for faith—and you will be in trouble.

It seems to me people ought to have a little sense. I do not understand how some people can go around spouting off things, endeavoring to believe, and calling it faith, when it is only presumption and folly. As a 15-year-old boy, just 4 months old in the Lord, I knew better than that.

For example, this is an account of the first step of faith I ever made in my life, after receiving salvation. I had been bedfast four months. (I stayed bedfast a total of sixteen months.) The doctor wanted me on a soft diet. Some of the things he wanted me to eat I did not like. I would almost have to hold my nose when they brought the food to me. Under normal circumstances, it would have made me sick to eat those foods, due to allergies and other things. Just the smell made me sick to my stomach.

So I would pray each time before I ate, "Now Lord, the doctor says I need this. It is the right kind of food. There is food value in it. It is valuable to my physical being. So I pray and claim by faith that this food will have no ill effect upon me. I will not be sick in any way, shape, form, or fashion." Then I ate it. I have been eating those same foods all these years since and they have never yet made me sick.

My faith worked. It worked because the Scriptures teach that food is sanctified by the Word of God and prayer (1 Tim. 4:4,5). It worked because this was something that was good and necessary.

Now I will relate a similar, yet entirely different situation to show you something.

From the time I was 4 until I was 15, I drank coffee. As a little boy, it had a lot of milk in it—but by the time I was 11, I was drinking coffee as strong as Grandpa drank.

I got up one morning and ate breakfast—the same things I had been eating for years. I drank my coffee—just like I always had. About the time I got up from the table, I had an attack of acute indigestion. I was so sick, it seemed like dying would be a relief. I could not figure out what it was.

The next morning the same thing happened just as soon as I finished breakfast. So I began to leave off things. I left off this—and I left off that—and I left off the other. As a last resort, I left off the coffee. The moment I did, everything was all right. I didn't have an attack.

Then I began to reason, *Maybe it was because I drank too much coffee on an empty stomach before I started eating breakfast.* So I ate breakfast first, and then drank my coffee. Again I was sick. Then I tried eating my breakfast and just sipping a little coffee along with it. Still I was sick. The only thing I could do was to leave off coffee entirely.

Now this coffee incident happened when I was staying with my other grandparents. When I became totally bedfast I came back to my mother's parents' home. This grandmother, not knowing of my experience, asked the doctor if I could have coffee.

"No, I don't want him to have coffee."

"He has drunk coffee all his life," she said.

"Well, if he has, then it would be all right to give him a cup of weak coffee at breakfast," the doctor said.

So they brought me a cup of weak coffee. I drank it. And I like to have died.

Someone might ask, "Why didn't you believe God?"

I had enough sense to know my faith would not work there. Coffee has no food value. The doctor didn't want me to have it in the first place.

I knew *on the inside*—just as a 15-year-old boy—that my faith would work on that food. It had food value. My body needed it. The doctor said so. I never even tried to get my faith to work on the coffee. I knew it would not work.

One winter night after a seminar meeting in Tulsa, my wife and I and some others were invited to someone's home to eat. On the way over in the car it was mentioned we were going to have chili. (Our hostess made chili that was out of this world!)

One man in the car spoke up and said, "I can't eat chili. What am I going to do? Are they having anything else?"

"No, they are not going to have anything else." We knew; we had sampled her chili before and had arranged this for that very reason.

This man said, "I have ulcers. I can't eat chili."

I said, "Brother, don't bother about it at all. I'll sanctify it, and you can eat all you want. It won't have any effect on you."

He told me years afterwards that he almost questioned it, but then he decided, *"No, I won't doubt it."* He said, "You know, Brother Hagin, I ate one bowl of chili. Then I ate another. I finally had three bowls of chili—and it never had any effect upon me. Not only that, but from that day to this, I never have had another symptom of an ulcerated stomach."

He had a right to believe for that.

Have enough sense to know where your faith will work—and where it won't work. And do not get out beyond the Word of God.

Beyond the Word?

You are in trouble when you get out beyond the Word of God. That's what bothers me about many of the things some people are teaching—"new revelations," and so forth.

A certain teacher visited one of my services one night. Someone conducting the meeting recognized him and asked him to say a few words. While he was on the platform talking I knew this in my spirit: *This man is not*

right. He's not for real. (Now I do not mean that we are to
have a spirit of criticism and fault-finding—we should not
have that—but I believe the Spirit of God will alert us and
save us from problems and trouble if we will listen to
Him.) Though this man was saved and filled with the
Spirit, I sensed in my spirit that he had gotten "off." (If you
do not listen to the Bible and stay with the Bible you can
get off.)

In the process of time this man was teaching some
meetings in a large city. A friend of mine, himself a Bible
teacher for more than 35 years, told me what happened.

He said to me, "I'm embarrassed, Brother Hagin, that I
could be so misled, so taken in. Most of the folks in my
Bible class attended his meetings. There were some things
that were not all together right all along, but I wanted to
give the man the benefit of the doubt. Then one night, that
poor fellow really got off on some things."

(He had been teaching for several weeks. Then he got
into this other. That's how they do. They lead you on, little
by little.)

My friend continued, "After that session was over, I
went up to him. I said, 'Now, Brother, I have been going
along with you on some minor things that didn't amount to
much anyhow, but that which you put out tonight (I held
my Bible up), you are going to have to show me from the
Bible. I can't find it in the Bible. You will have to give me
chapter and verse, or I'm not going to accept it.' "

This man said to him, "Oh, you'll not find what I'm
teaching in that thing. I'm way out beyond that. I know
much more than what's in there."

When they know so much more than what's in the
Bible, they are too far out for me. No man who had any

respect for God would ever call the Bible a "thing." Yet people were misled.

My friend, a Bible teacher of more than 35 years, said to me, "What I hate about it, Brother Hagin, is that when I tried to pull my group out—we'd cooperated with the meetings—I lost a lot of them. They were carried off."

A little Chinese woman who had been Buddhist most of her life was not carried off—yet she was only four months old in the Lord when this happened.

Her parents had come over from the old country when she was a little girl. They went into business. She and her sister took over the business when the parents became aged. The mother had become bedfast. Doctors could not help her. They prayed to Buddha—they had a statue of Buddha worth thousands of dollars in the basement of their beautiful home—but the old mother did not get healed. They read about a healing revival going on in town (it was at the church where my friend, the Bible teacher of 35 years, taught a large Bible class) and decided to carry the old woman to that meeting. She received healing and salvation. The young Chinese woman was born again— then she got her father and her sister saved.

As a new baby, she went with my friend's Bible class to this series of meetings. She told me when I was in that church holding meetings some time later, "The first time I heard that fellow, something on the inside of me said, *'Leave that fellow alone. Don't go back to hear him anymore. He's false.'* "

Think about it. These older Christians, some of them saved and filled with the Holy Spirit 35 years and more, were taken in. A baby, not even Spirit-filled, knew the difference. The others swallowed it —and got all messed up. Isn't that tragic?

There is no need for such a thing happening if we will just learn to listen to our hearts, our spirits.

That's what the little Chinese woman did. Though she was only four months old in the Lord, *on the inside of her* she just knew that something was wrong. And what she heard him teach the night she was there might not even have been so wrong—it was later that he began to put out a lot of false stuff.

I knew, just as a youngster only 4 months old in the Lord, that my faith would not work on coffee. So I didn't try to make it work. I knew it would work on the food.

Presumption

Be certain that the promises of God cover what you are believing for. You have a right to believe for anything God's Word promises you. But if you get out beyond that—then you are out on presumption, or foolishness.

For instance, sometimes single people, because "you can have what you say," will pick out someone and claim them as a mate.

They have a right—because there is Scripture for it—to claim a wife or husband. But they do not necessarily have the right just to pick somebody out and say, "I'm going to claim him, or her." That person has something to do with it. They have the right to believe God for a wife or husband—but they should let the Lord send them one.

A young graduate from a denominational seminary was in some of our meetings in Texas. He had been filled with the Holy Spirit and had been kicked out of his denomination. He took my wife and me out for lunch one day where he announced, "I'm getting married."

"Oh," my wife said, "who is the lucky girl?"

He proceeded to tell us about a woman who sang in the choir at the church he now attended. He did not even know her name. He had never met her. He just liked the looks of her sitting up there in the choir.

He said, "I claimed her. Brother Hagin preaches you can have what you say. I've already said it."

My wife asked, "And you never even have had a date with her?"

"No. I never have shaken her hand, or even seen her up close."

Well, when he got up close, she might not have looked as good as she did from a distance. Besides that, she would have something to say about it. He cannot override her will.

He has a right to claim a wife. The Bible says, *"Whoso findeth a wife findeth a good thing, and obtaineth favour of the Lord"* (Prov. 18:22). He has a right to claim a wife—but he should let God bring him the one He wants for him.

I started preaching when I was 17. It seemed as if someone was always trying to make a match for me. One girl came and told me that God showed her she was supposed to marry me. "Well," I said, "when He tells me, I will accept it." He never did tell me.

Such things would be funny if they were not so pathetic. Lives have been ruined over things like that.

Foundation for Faith

Be sure the Scriptures cover what you are believing for. Do not get out beyond God's Word.

Through the years many people have come to me saying something similar to this, "Brother Hagin, I want you to pray with me about this . . . . "

I purposely ask them, "What Scriptures are you standing on?"

Eight out of ten times—and I kept a record of it for years—they looked at me with a blank expression and said, "Well, not any in particular."

I said, "That's what you will get—nothing in particular. You have no foundation for faith. Faith is based on what God said. Faith in God is faith in God's Word."

Many times we use terms loosely. Recognize that when we talk about faith, we are talking about faith in God— and faith in God is faith in His Word. " . . . *faith cometh by hearing, and hearing by the word of God"* (Rom. 10:17). You are not going to have faith for something if you do not hear the Word of God on it.

Recognize and realize that. Find Scriptures that cover your case. Find the Scriptures that promise you the things you are praying for. Then you have a solid foundation for faith.

If something arises—even though I know the Scriptures which apply and can quote many of them—I do not pray about the matter immediately. I go to the Word. I read again the same Scriptures I could quote. I go over them, and over them, and over them—sometimes for a day or two. (Now if an emergency arises that is a different thing.) I go over them again, and again, and again. In doing that I am building the Word of God into my spirit-consciousness. Then, when I get ready to act in faith, *there is no doubt.* I am solid.

I do not want to attract attention to myself—I tell this

to glorify God and His Word—not one single time in more than 50 years have I had a prayer go unanswered. (Now you understand I am talking about things concerning myself individually. When you are praying about someone else, their will enters in.) As far as me individually, I never prayed about anything without getting it.

Sometimes it would take a little time. I just stayed in the Word every moment I could. I would meditate for hours on the Scriptures that covered what I was believing for. Then I believed only that. I had a sure foundation for faith.

Sometimes I had to make adjustments before the answer could manifest. I made them in a hurry. For instance, in 1949, I left the last church I pastored and went out into a field ministry at the Lord's direction. At the end of my first year of traveling, I spent three days fasting and praying about it. I reminded the Lord of something He said in the Old Testament: *"If ye be willing and obedient, ye shall eat the good of the land"* (Isa. 1:19).

(That Scripture belongs to us, too. We can prove from the New Testament that we fell heir to it. It means that you will prosper and have things good. It does not mean you will never have any tests—because the devil will put pressure on you.)

I told the Lord, "Lord, my children are not even eating right. I've worn out my car; now I'm out here on the field on foot. I'm sure not eating the good of the land—yet You promised that. Something is wrong somewhere." (I knew the trouble was with me. The problem is never with God.)

The third day of my fast, just as plainly as somebody speaking, the Lord said, "That text you keep quoting to me says, 'If you be willing and obedient.' You were obedient, but you were not willing. You do not qualify. That is the reason it is not working for you."

(I kept trying to magnify the obedience part—He got on the willing part. You can actually obey the Lord, just like a child can obey his parents and not be willing, and miss it.)

I got willing in 10 seconds. Don't tell me it takes a long time. It didn't take me 10 seconds to make a little adjustment right down on the inside.

Then I said, "Lord, I'm ready now. You already told me that I was obedient. Now I am willing. I know it. You know it. And the devil knows it. So I'm ready now to start eating the good."

He said, "Yes, you are. Now I will tell you what to do."

He told me, and I've been eating the good ever since.

Walking in the Light

The psalmist of old said, *"The entrance of thy words giveth light . . . ."* (Ps. 119:130). The entrance of God's Word gives light.

When there is light in a room, it is no problem at all to walk around in it. But with all the lights out on a dark night, you may stumble and fall over objects in that room. As long as the light is there, you can walk fine.

The entrance of His Words gives light. The reason many fall and fail is because they have left the light of the Word of God. They are walking in presumption or folly.

What does God's Word say?

Too many answer, "Well, I don't know."

Find out what it says. Find the Scriptures that promise you the things you are praying for. You are always on safe ground when you are on the Scriptures. When you get away from them, you are in a gray area.

Some people want to step over into the dark—and whether or not the Word of God promises it, they say, "I'm just going to believe."

Believing God is believing His Word. Oh, how necessary it is to know the Word of God. Thank God, He has given us His Word. We need not be in the dark. The entrance of His Word gives light.

What does it mean to walk in the light? It means to walk in the Word! Walking in the Word is walking in the light. To walk away from the Word means to walk into darkness.

Confessions: (Say these aloud)

I am a believer.
I am not a doubter.
I do have faith.
My faith works.
My faith is in God the Father.
My faith is in the Lord Jesus Christ.
My faith is in the Holy Bible, the Word of God.
God's Word is true.
I believe the Word of God.
Therefore, I believe God.
God's Word works!

Step Three: Be sure you are not living in sin—practicing wrongdoing.

The Bible says, *"If we walk in the light, as he is in the light, we have fellowship one with another, and the blood of Jesus Christ his Son cleanseth us from all sin"* (1 John 1:7).

What does it mean to walk in the light? It means to walk in the Word.

As long as you walk in what light you have, there is an automatic cleansing from all sin by the blood of Jesus Christ.

But if you persist in living in wrongdoing, you are going to get into trouble sooner or later. Your faith will not work. Your prayers will not work.

Sin: Hindrance to Faith

Jesus spoke these great words on the subject of faith: *"Whosoever shall say unto this mountain, Be thou removed,*

and be thou cast into the sea; and shall not doubt in his
heart, but shall believe that those things which he saith
shall come to pass; he shall have whatsoever he saith.
Therefore I say unto you, What things soever ye desire,
when ye pray, believe that ye receive them, and ye shall have
them." He went right on to say, *"And when ye stand*
praying, forgive, if ye have aught against any: that your
Father also which is in heaven may forgive you your
trespasses" (Mark 11:25). He was talking about a
hindrance to faith and prayer.

If there is an air of "unforgiveness" about you, your
faith won't work. Your prayers won't work.

If my faith and my prayers were not working, this
would be the first place I would look. But I never permit
the least bit of ill will or hard feelings in my heart against
anybody. I absolutely refuse it.

Of course, the devil will suggest things to your head—
but you are not to walk by your head. You walk by your
heart. Thoughts may come and they may persist in
staying. But thoughts that are not put into word or action
die unborn.

You need to know that. Because the devil, endeavoring
to defeat you, will put thoughts in your mind. Then he will
tell you, "If you were saved, you would never have thought
such a thing as that." So, let me say it again: *Thoughts*
may come. Thoughts may persist in staying. But thoughts
that are not put into words or actions die unborn.

A fellow holding a meeting for me when I was still
pastoring created some problems. He did some things
which were wrong. There was no doubt about it. The
thought came to me (I recognized it was the devil putting it
into my mind—anything that is defeat, anything nega-

tive, anything the least bit wrong is the devil): *After all he's done, if I were you, I just wouldn't take him up another offering. I would just wait until Sunday night, and then I wouldn't do much for him.*

I said, "Devil, if you don't shut up, I will take up two offerings every night." (I already was passing the plate every night and saying, "This is going to the evangelist.") Boy, he hushed in a hurry. He doesn't want any preacher to get two offerings a night.

I went out of my way to be extra kind to this man. The Bible teaches us to return good for evil (Matt. 5:44). I knew that he went mostly to larger churches than mine. I asked him what his average offerings were. Then I saw to it that he got 'way beyond his average—and I put in a lot of it myself. I am going to return good for evil. I am not going to allow any kind of animosity, ill will, or wrong feelings.

We are so in the natural that we get oriented to the natural. When we think about sin, we think about sins of the flesh—robbing a bank, committing adultery, and so on. We think, *Oh, isn't that terrible!* And it is. But God will judge you quicker on spiritual sins than on physical sins. I know—because Jesus said that to me one time when He appeared to me. It shocked me.

A lot of times you can get by for a while with some physical sins—but God will judge you quicker on spiritual sins.

We cannot see the attitude of someone's heart—but God can. People can act right on the outside, when on the inside—oh, brother! God sees all of that.

Balance in Self-Examination

There is a need for balance in this area.

Some people let the devil harass them about wrongdoing, past mistakes, past failures, past sins. This robs them of their faith, robs them of their healing, robs them of the blessings God intended they should have.

If we look back, we can all see where we have missed it. Hindsight is better than foresight. Sometimes, at the moment, we thought we were doing well. Then, as we look back, we almost get embarrassed. I pastored nearly 12 years. I left some churches to go pastor another church thinking I had done an excellent job. But after I grew a little spiritually and looked back, I almost hid my face in shame. It is certainly true, that as we look back, we can allow the devil to defeat us.

A businessman in the church where I was holding a meeting needed healing. His condition was desperate, incurable. Doctors had advised him to sell his business. They said if he did not, he would be dead within six months. The best they could offer was that if he sold his business, stayed on medication, and rested he might live two years.

He had been in several healing meetings. The most outstanding healing evangelists had laid hands on him. I laid hands on him several times. But he had not received his healing.

He wanted to talk with me. I agreed to meet him in the pastor's office before the next evening's service.

While I was shaving, getting ready to go, on the inside of me I heard, "Do you think I would require you to do something I wouldn't do?" I let that get by me at first, went on shaving, and got my mind off on something else. Again,

on the inside, in my spirit, there was this inward voice, "Do
you think I would require you to do something I wouldn't
be willing to do?" I let it get by me the second time.

Then, as I was putting on my coat to head for the
church, again on the inside of me, this inward voice said,
"Do you think I would require you to do something I
wouldn't be willing to do?"

I recognized it as the Lord.

I answered aloud, "Certainly not. You wouldn't require
us to do something You wouldn't be willing to do. That
would be unjust. It would be wrong." I thought no more
about it.

I got into my car and headed toward the church. As I
was driving along, thinking about my evening's message,
again on the inside of me, He said, "Remember what I said
to Peter when he asked, 'Lord, how oft shall my brother sin
against me, and I forgive him? till seven times?' I said, 'Not
seven times, but until seventy times seven.' That is 490
times—and all of it in one day."

I had read that hundreds of times, but it had never
really dawned on me that way.

Then this inward voice said, "James 5 says, *'Is any sick
among you? let him call for the elders of the church; and let
them pray over him, anointing him with oil in the name of
the Lord: And the prayer of faith shall save the sick, and the
Lord shall raise him up;* (We always quote that part of this
Scripture—but this inward voice quoted the rest of it.) *and
if he have committed sins, they shall be forgiven
him' "* (vv. 14,15).

I wondered why the Lord was talking to me this way.
But as soon as I got to the pastor's office and this
businessman started talking, I understood.

He told me he had been saved and baptized in the Holy Spirit for 37 years. Then he said, "Now, Brother Hagin, I'll tell you just why my faith doesn't work." He stood there and talked himself, me, and God out of his healing. He was just sure God wouldn't heal anybody like him. "Because," he said, "as I look back over these 37 years, I've failed in so many ways."

I saw what the Lord was doing. He was giving me Scripture to give to this man.

I asked him, "What terrible sins have you committed? How many banks have you robbed? How many lies have you told?"

He said, "They are not sins of commission—they are mostly sins of omission. I've made good money through these 37 years. I could have done more than just pay tithes. Sometimes I didn't even do that. I could have put more money into the church. I could have given more money to missions. I could have prayed more. In my business I could have witnessed more for God."

I gave him the Scriptures the Lord gave me, laid hands on him there in the study, and he was completely healed.

Twenty years later I was preaching in that part of the country. Somebody told me he had just retired at 82. He had been about to let the devil defeat him because of past mistakes, past failures, and past wrongdoing. But I said to him that night in the pastor's study, "You asked the Lord to forgive you, didn't you?"

"Yes."

I said, "He forgave you. Praise God, they are all gone. Don't drag them up."

On The Other Hand

Now—right on the other hand—if you persist in continuing to practice sin and wrongdoing, you are going to get into trouble. If you do not judge yourself, God, sooner or later, will have to judge you.

> **1 CORINTHIANS 11:31**
> **31 For if we would judge ourselves, we should not be judged.**

How do we judge ourselves?

If we do wrong, we face up to it and say, "That is wrong. I judge that. I am going to put that away and not do it anymore." We judge ourselves and refuse to practice, or to live in, sin anymore.

And oh, the grace of God! I don't know whether any of us has really plumbed the depth of His grace. I have seen it in manifestation until I have gone away weeping.

Years ago, an older gentleman in our city was desperately ill. I was traveling in a field ministry; he requested that I come by and see him when I got home. Now he did not ask me to pray for his healing. He just wanted me to pray with him. The presence of God met us in a marvelous way.

But somehow, when I would try to make my tongue say healing, it would not. It was as though something had hold of my tongue. It would not say healing. I would think healing, but my tongue would not say what I was thinking. I could not pray for his healing.

I went back another time, at his request, to pray for him. Doctors now said it was just a matter of time—he might live a few months. (He did live two months after this.) Standing at his bedside with my hand on his head, I tried to pray for his healing—but my tongue would not say what I was thinking.

I took my hand off his head. In my spirit I said, "Lord, why can't I pray for this man's healing? After all, he's not 70 years old yet. You promised us at least 70 or 80 years. (That should be a minimum—and you can go on up, according to how much you can believe for.) Why? Why? Why?"

Just as plainly, on the inside of me, the Lord said (and I did not know these things; it came by revelation), "I have been waiting on him 36 years. He is 66 years old; he was born again when he was 30. I have been waiting on him 36 years to judge himself and to put away wrongdoing. He never has lived right over two weeks at a time in 36 years. I have been waiting on him to judge himself and to put away sin. But he would not do it. So I have turned him over to Satan for the destruction of the flesh that his spirit may be saved in the day of the Lord Jesus."

Another man, only 43 years old, had cancer of both lungs. His sister, a Full Gospel pastor's wife, called me to pray for him when he took a turn for the worse.

I laid my hand on his head to pray and shut my eyes. It felt as if somebody laid their hand on mine and took my hand off his head. As I continued to pray, I thought to myself, *I was pressing too hard. He must have taken my hand off his head.* So I put my hand back on his head, shut my eyes, and continued to pray. Again, I felt that hand on my hand. It took my hand off his head. I still was praying, but thinking this on the inside, *I don't think I was pressing too hard.* So this time I put my hand back on his head and kept my eyes open. I continued to pray. I did not see any hand—it was not the man who did it—but I could feel, just as real as though some person did it, a hand on my hand which took my hand off his head.

When that happened, while still praying in English out of my mind, in my spirit down inside, I said, "Lord, why did You take my hand off his head?"

He said, "Because he is going to die. Do not pray for him."

I said, "Lord, he is only 43 years old. You promised us at least 70 or 80 years, or even longer. He is not old enough to die. Why should he die?"

He said, "I have been waiting on him for 30 years to judge himself and put away sin. He was saved when he was 13. Thirty years I have been waiting on him."

Think about the patience of God. We get so impatient with one another. Sometimes I get sort of impatient with people. (You never do, do you?) And then I get to thinking about it like this, *I've just got to put up with this little thing. But God is putting up with all of us.* Then I repent and go on.

Think about the longsuffering of God. He said, "I have been waiting on him to judge himself for 30 years. He never has lived right in all these 30 years. He persisted in doing wrong. In fact, I healed him of a broken back one time when he was living in adultery."

(I knew none of this. It came by revelation. But I asked his sister about it later and she told me it was all true. She told me, "Yes, he had left his wife and was living with another woman when on the job he fell and broke his back. When he could leave the hospital he came back to our home. I was only 12; I helped Mother take care of him. He was in a cast from his neck down. He knew how to pray. So he got to praying and told us that the Lord had healed him. He wanted to cut off the cast. The doctors said, 'No! If you cut off that cast, you will turn black and blue and die.' But once when everybody was gone, he got me to bring a butcher knife. He helped me cut off that cast. He got up out of bed and did just what the doctor said—turned black and fell on the floor. But then, just suddenly, he rose up perfectly well.")

The Lord said to me, "He continued to live on in sin. But now he has everything fixed up spiritually. He has everything fixed up financially. He has everything ready. He will never have a better time to go. Let him come on home."

(That was not the best God had for him. He missed God's best. I don't want to miss God's best. I don't want to take second best—or third best—or fourth best—or fifth best. I want the best! Don't you?)

Then the Lord said, "He will be dead in two days."

I went my way. I told his brother-in-law, the Full Gospel pastor, that the Lord said he would be dead within two days.

The next day, one of the man's doctors came out and ate Sunday dinner with them. The man was up and around; he went to the table to eat.

He asked his doctor, "How much time do I have left?"

The doctor said, "Oh, you don't have to worry about dying for another six months or so. Medical science is working constantly; maybe we will come up with something. Don't give up hope."

He said, "Doctor, it might interest you to know that I am going home tomorrow night at 10:20."

Someone told his brother-in-law, the pastor, what he

had said. After a meeting at the church was over about
9:30 on Sunday night, the pastor and his wife drove by her
brother's house. He was sitting out on the front porch on
the porch swing.

"He waved at us," the pastor told me later. "I pulled up
my car to the front of the house and my wife talked to him
from the car. Then we said, 'We'll see you tomorrow.' He
just said, 'Bye-bye.' When we got home the phone was
ringing. They told us he had died about one minute before.
He went home at 10:20 just like he said."

I am glad he went home. I am glad he is up there
walking up and down the streets of gold. But I am sorry he
missed out on God's best.

Now, what am I saying to you?

I am saying, do not wait until you get into trouble.
Correct yourself right now if you are living in sin—if you
are persisting in wrongdoing. Do not let anything touch
you that is wrong—physical sins (sins of the flesh) or
spiritual sins (sins of the spirit).

After being baptized in the Holy Spirit as a Baptist
pastor, and receiving the left foot of fellowship from among
the Baptists, I accepted the pastorate of a little Full Gospel
church in north-central Texas. I had been pastor of this
church three months when a woman came to the par-
sonage one August day in 1939.

"Brother Hagin," she said, "I've got a question for you."

She looked so serious, I braced myself and got ready for
it.

First, she told me about her family. "Now I just got
saved eight months before you came here. But my mother
and the rest of my family have been in this church for 23
years. They are wonderful Christians. No one has been

more faithful than they. They came every service. They paid their tithes."

I said, "Yes, that is right." They were the most faithful family in the church—and spiritual.

Then she told me about her husband's family. "You didn't know my husband's family. They moved away before you got here. They are good people; don't misunderstand me. They wouldn't lie for anything in the world. But they were not as faithful as they should have been about coming to church."

She went on, "Now I have been watching my side of the family for 23 years, and if any of my family ever got healed, I don't know it. Our family members always wind up going to the hospital, being operated on, or dying."

(Her mother was one of the most spiritual persons I ever met—a marvelous, deeply spiritual woman. Gifts of the Spirit operated through her. You are not going to get healed, however, just because gifts of the Spirit operate through you.)

"But in my husband's family, in a 23-year period, if one of them ever failed to get healed, I don't know it."

I said, "Mary, you haven't asked me anything; you have told me something."

"Well," she said, "here is my question. How come?"

"I don't know," I said.

You cannot say why some people get healed and some do not, unless God gives you a specific revelation. In fact, Jesus said to me once when He appeared to me in a vision and I asked Him about one of my own loved ones who failed to receive healing, "That is none of your business. It is between me and that person. If I wanted you to know, I would have told you. I did not tell you so I did not want you to know. Did you ever read in my Book, 'The secret things belong unto the Lord our God: but those things which are revealed belong unto us and to our children for ever'?"

I said, "Yes, that's Deuteronomy 29:29."

"Well," He said, "if I had revealed it to you, I would have wanted you to know. I did not, so don't even touch it in thought life."

So I didn't even think about it any more. I just forgot it.

(Some people are sticking their noses into other people's business. They run around saying, "Why didn't so-and-so get healed?" It is none of their business; it is God's business. If He wanted them to know, He would have told them. If He did not tell them, they should forget it.)

In that same vision Jesus said to me, "Keep preaching the Word. Whether your relatives get it or not, it does not do away with the Word."

You see, the Word of God is revealed to us. What it reveals belongs to us and our children forever.

"I don't know specifically," I told Mary, "why one family always received healing, and one did not. But I do know the Bible. And because I do know the Bible, I know that people who get results follow the Word of God. So I would say this.

"I would say that your husband's family had two characteristics. Number one—and there are two points to this first one—I would say they were always quick to forgive and quick to repent. Number two, they were always quick to believe."

Figuratively speaking, Mary's eyes got almost as big as saucers. She said, "Brother Hagin, you have hit the nail on the head."

I said, "No, I didn't. Jesus did. I got that out of the

Book."

She said, "I believe my husband's people are the quickest people in the world, when they see they are wrong, to repent and just quit whatever it may be. They are the quickest people, when they see they have done you wrong, to ask you to forgive them. They are the most forgiving people—and they are sincere. And they are the quickest people to believe God I have seen.

"But now," she said, "you take Momma and us. Our whole family is this way—and most of the others have been saved, filled with the Spirit, and faithful Christians for years. We will forgive you, eventually, because we know we have to; the Bible says so. But we hold out to the end. All of us are that way. That's just our nature."

(It wasn't their spiritual nature. They received a new nature when they were born again. It was their physical nature. All of us have certain natural physical characteristics which we let dominate us, if we are not careful.)

"Just at the last moment," she went on, "when we see we have to, we'll forgive you. And when it comes to believing, we are the slowest people you have ever seen to believe anybody, or anything, including God."

I think that some folks delight in living right on the edge of disaster—and once in a while they fall over. God does not want us to live there.

Be quick to forgive

Be quick to repent.

Be quick to believe God.

1 JOHN 3:21
21 Beloved, if our heart condemn us not, then have we confidence toward God.

If you are doing wrong, you know it. Right on the inside of yourself—in your heart—you know it. If you do not know it—if your heart does not condemn you—forget it.

Now if you listen to some people, you will always be under condemnation. Everything, according to them, is wrong. Someone wrote us a note during one of our crusades to this effect: "This is not of God. God isn't using you (talking about our entire crusade team) because you wear jewelry and the women don't have long hair." Do not allow yourself to come under condemnation because of everybody's ideas. It will keep your faith from working.

In one of my meetings, I laid hands on a woman and prayed with her. She had been filled with the Holy Spirit and speaking with tongues about 15 minutes—just having a great time—when she had to stop and sit down on the altar. She was sitting there with her hands raised, praising God in English, when a man who had been praying with the men in another place came over that way. He heard her praying to God in English and supposed she had not received. He went up to her and said, "Sister, pull off that wedding band and God will fill you with the Holy Ghost."

I quickly got hold of him and ushered him away, saying, "Brother, God already has filled her with the Holy Ghost—wedding band and all."

Running the Race

The Bible talks about sin. It also talks about weights.

HEBREWS 12:1
1 Wherefore seeing we also are compassed about with so great a cloud of witnesses, let us lay aside

every WEIGHT, and the SIN which doth so easily beset us, and let us run with patience the race that is set before us.

Sin, the Bible says, is a transgression of the law (1 John 3:4). We will have to determine in our own hearts the things that are weights to us. What would be a weight to me might not be a weight to you. We will have to lay aside those things if we are going to run with patience the race that is set before us.

Now I am not talking about trying to do what everybody says—that would keep you almost constantly jumping. Folks let that bring them under condemnation and it keeps their faith from working.

I am talking about what your own spirit tells you. If you are a child of God, in your own spirit, in your own heart, right down on the inside of you, you know the minute you miss it. (Sometimes people say, "Well, if I know my heart .... " Don't put an "if" in it. You know your heart.)

Don't wait—don't even wait until you come to church—just stop right then and say, "Lord, I missed it. I failed. Forgive me." And He will do it.

That is judging yourself.

Step Four: Be sure no doubt or unbelief is permitted in your life concerning the promises of God.

Understand this—you have already taken Step Two. Step Two, you remember is: *Be sure the promises of God, the Scriptures, cover the thing you are believing for.* Therefore, you should have no doubt about it. If it is in God's Word, it belongs to you.

If anything is trying to keep you from having it, that is the devil and not God. Satan, as we have seen, is the god of this world (2 Cor. 4:4). Many of the things we believe for and pray about, which the promises of God cover, have to come to pass in this world where Satan is god. He will do everything in the world to keep it from coming. This does not mean God doesn't hear you the first time you pray—nor that the answer is not on the way.

In Daniel we have a good illustration of this. Daniel set himself to seek God. He fasted. He was not on what we call a total fast, however; he ate no "pleasant bread" for 21 days.

days.

God sent an angel with the answer—but the angel was 21 days in getting through. He told Daniel, *"For from the first day that thou didst set thine heart to understand, and to chasten thyself before thy God, thy words were heard, and I am come for thy words"* (Dan. 10:12).

God did not send the answer the 21st day. He sent the answer the first day.

What happened? The angel told Daniel, *" . . . the prince of the kingdom of Persia withstood me one and twenty days"* (v. 13). This prince of Persia did not want the angel to get through with the answer.

What Satan said to Jesus at the temptation, when he took Him up into a high mountain and showed Him all the kingdoms of the world in a moment of time, was a real temptation. The devil said, *"All this power will I give thee, and the glory of them: for that is delivered unto me; and to whomsoever I will I give it"* (Luke 4:6).

The prince of Persia was over in the spirit world where evil spirits were ruling that nation. Those spirits did not want the angel to get through with the answer.

God heard Daniel the first day. God sent the answer the first day. God sent the answer when you prayed, too. It may not have materialized yet, but He sent the answer right then, when you prayed.

Many people, if the answer does not materialize right away, drop back into unbelief and doubt. They say, "Maybe it wasn't the will of God to begin with."

The only child of one family, a little girl, had been afflicted all her life. Her mother, new in the charismatic move, carried the child to several ministers for prayer. For some reason, the child did not receive her healing. Then the mother said, "It's just not the will of God. I took her and had her prayed for. If it had been God's will, He would have healed her. He didn't. So it is not the will of God."

No—it was the will of God to heal that child! Such thinking violates the promises of God. Healing belonged to the child. Healing belonged to the family. Healing belonged to the mother—but she let doubt and unbelief come in concerning the promises of God, and it robbed her of the blessings God intended she should have.

No—if God said it, He intended we should have it! He would not provide something for us and then put it under lock and key and not let us have it.

Realize that it is not God who is withholding it from you. It is the devil who is hindering you and trying to keep it from manifesting.

So stand your ground. Be certain no doubt or unbelief is permitted in your life concerning the promises of God. Constantly confess and confirm that God's Word is true.

God's Word is true!

It Shall Be
Even As It Was Told Me

I like something Paul said on board that tempest-tossed ship.

If they had listened to him they would not have gotten into trouble to begin with, because when they boarded he said, *"Sirs, I perceive that this voyage will be with hurt and much damage, not only of the lading and ship, but also of our lives"* (Acts 27:10).

Paul just had that *perception* in his spirit. I have had that, too—many times. Sometimes I did not pay attention to it like I should have. Thank God, He will have mercy on us anyway.

They lost the ship. They lost the merchandise. They would have lost their lives—but Paul said: *"Be of good cheer: for there shall be no loss of any man's life among you, but of the ship. For there stood by me this night the angel of God, **whose I am,** and **whom I serve,** Saying, Fear not, Paul; thou must be brought before Caesar: and, lo, God hath given thee all them that sail with thee. Wherefore, sirs, be of good cheer: for **I believe God,** that it shall be even as it was told me"* (Acts 27:22-25).

Paul made three positive statements that bless me.

1. I belong to God. That's a good thing to know, isn't it? He was in the midst of danger, in the midst of a storm, in the midst of trial, but he did not forget that he belonged to God. He said, *". . . the angel of God, **whose I am.**"* I belong to God! To whom do you belong?

2. I serve God. Somebody said, "I'm trying to." No, you are to do it. I serve God.

3. I believe God. Paul said, *"I believe God, that it shall be even as it was told me."* Somebody said, "Oh, but an angel appeared to Paul." The Word of God tells us that we have a more sure and steadfast Word in this Book—the Bible—than in the word of an angel.

Paul's statements have brought me through many a hard place. I just simply stood my ground and said, "Wherefore, sirs (to the devil and anybody else who would listen), I belong to God. I serve God. And I believe God. I believe God that it shall be even as it was told me."

I was talking about even as it was told me in the Book—the Bible. I believe it shall be even as it was told me!

We all go through the hard places of life. The crises of life come to all of us. We are not immune to them. Satan is the god of this world. He is the one who sends the trials. It isn't God. It is the devil putting pressure on us. He wants to find out if we really believe what we claim to believe.

He will try to find out right away. He wants to steal truth. I have told people, after a series of teaching services, "Get ready for it. As soon as the meeting is over the devil will put on the pressure. Tests and trials are coming. He will endeavor to rob you. If he can get you wallowing in unbelief, he will rob you of the truth God was trying to get over to you. If he is successful, then he can keep you defeated the rest of your life."

A Doer of the Word

People misinterpret what Jesus was teaching about the houses built on rock or sand. Jesus said . . . .

MATTHEW 7:24-27
24 Therefore WHOSOEVER HEARETH THESE SAYINGS OF MINE, AND DOETH THEM, I will liken him unto a wise man, which built his house upon a rock:
25 And the rain descended, and the floods came, and the winds blew, and beat upon that house; and it fell not: for it was founded upon a rock.
26 And EVERY ONE THAT HEARETH THESE SAYINGS OF MINE, AND DOETH THEM NOT, shall be likened unto a foolish man, which built his house upon the sand:
27 And the rain descended, and the floods came, and the winds blew, and beat upon that house; and it fell.

The same storm came. The same rains fell. The same floods came. The same winds blew. One house fell. One did not fall because it was founded upon a rock.

Some say, "Jesus is the Rock—and I'm built on Jesus."

No, we see people who are saved and built on Jesus, the Rock, going down everywhere. That is not what Jesus is saying in this passage. Jesus is talking about *being a doer of the Word*.

It is the one who *does* the Word of God who stands. The *doer* of the Word is the person who stands!

The Good Fight

It is not always the easiest thing in the world to live the faith life. There is a fight to it. The Bible plainly says, *"Fight the good fight of faith . . . ."* (1 Tim. 6:12).

I think some people read the first word, "Fight," quit right there, and started fighting. Some must think it said, "Fight other churches and fellow Christians."

I have seen preachers pull off their coat, loosen their tie, roll up their sleeves, and say, "I'm going to fight the devil." I thought to myself as I sat there, *They wouldn't be any match for him. Why do they want to fight him anyway? Jesus already has defeated him.*

I have seen them go through the same motions and declare, "I'm going to fight sin." Again, I thought, *Why do they want to do that? Jesus already has cured it. He put it away.*

Jesus put away sin by the sacrifice of Himself (Heb. 9:26). There is no sin problem—there is a sinner problem. Get the sinner to Jesus and that cures that. He already has cured the sin problem.

We used to see signs and advertising campaigns saying, "Help Fight Polio." Then they found a vaccine. So we don't see that now. They are not fighting polio anymore; they have something for it. We still see signs and campaigns asking for money to help fight cancer. They have not yet found a cure for cancer.

There is no use in fighting sin—Jesus is the cure! Don't preach sin—preach the Cure!

What fight are we supposed to get into? The good fight of faith!

Notice the word *good*. It does not say, "Fight the bad fight of faith," or, "the evil fight of faith."

Keep that in mind while we go way back in the Bible to when Israel came out of Egypt and up to the border of Canaan's land. From a place called Kadesh-barnea, they sent 12 spies to spy out the land. The Bible says that 10 of the 12 brought back an *evil* report (Num. 13:32). Their report was a report of doubt. "There are giants in the land," they said. "We are as grasshoppers in their sight. We can't take the land." The Bible calls their report an evil report. It was a report of doubt.

Two of the spies, Caleb and Joshua, brought back a *good* report. What was their good report? "Sure the giants are there," they said. They did not deny that fact. "Sure in our own eyes we are as grasshoppers in their sight . . . BUT! . . . our God is WELL ABLE to deliver them into our hands! Let us go up at once and possess it!"

Faith always has a *good* report. Now come on over in the New Testament to First Timothy 6:12, *"Fight the good fight of faith . . . ."*

You have to fight to maintain a *good* report. It is not easy to do so when the giants are standing there looking you in the face and you look like a grasshopper in their sight. Yet you must maintain a good report. The only thing that will put you over is maintaining that good report.

Fight the *good* fight!

Faith always has a *good* report!

If you have any other kind of report which is not good, then you are not in the faith fight.

"How are you doing?"

"Well, I woke up this morning with my lumbago giving me fits. I told John before he went to work, 'I've had everybody to pray. I've gotten in Brother Hagin's healing line. I guess it's just not God's will to heal me. You know, it just doesn't ever work for us.' "

That is not a good report.

In the face of seeming defeat—when faith seems weak and victory seems lost—fight the good fight of faith! Fight to maintain a good report. Do not tell people how you feel. Do not tell people about your aches and pains.

"How are things?" they may ask.

Answer with a good report, "Bless God, God is on our side. Greater is He that is in me than he that is in the world. Jesus took my infirmities and bare my sicknesses."

Get in on the right fight. Fight the good fight of faith. You have to fight to maintain a good report right in the face of adverse circumstances.

I was in St. Louis at a Full Gospel Business Men's convention, teaching on faith in the afternoons. A woman stopped me in the foyer of the hotel where the meetings were held and asked if she could speak to me.

She said, "I want you to promise me something."

I said, "I won't promise something when I don't know what it is."

She began to cry. She said, "I'm a widow. I have a 15½-year-old son. And, Brother Hagin, I can't do a thing with him. He won't go to church. He runs with a gang and sometimes he doesn't get in until 3 or 4 o'clock in the morning. I'm afraid he is going to get involved with dope. I lie awake at night just waiting for the phone to ring and someone to tell me he's been arrested. I want you to promise me you will pray for him every day."

I said, "I'm not going to do it." I said it purposely to get her attention.

She looked at me, startled, and said, "You're not?"

I said, "No, I'm not. In fact, I'm not going to pray for him at all—not one single prayer."

"Well," she said. Her eyes grew big. I had been preaching on faith and prayer.

I explained, "You see, it wouldn't do any good. You would nullify the effects of all my praying. You would keep on telling him he never is going to amount to anything— he never will make it—he'll wind up in a reform school, or the penitentiary."

She said, "How did you know I had been talking that way?"

I said, "Because he turned out that way. That's the reason he did. You have been saying the wrong things. You didn't have the right report."

She said, "What am I to do?"

I said, "When he was small you should have trained him. Now, this has gone on so long, you must leave him alone. Get off his back."

She said, "When he was small I wasn't even saved myself. I didn't go to church."

I said, "Don't even ask him to go. He resents it. He has

gone so far now, you had better leave him alone. Quit nagging him. Don't say to him one single time, 'You're going to the reform school,' or, 'You're going to wind up in the penitentiary,' or, 'You never will make it,' or, 'You're a bad boy.'

"And at night, when he is gone and you don't know where he is, quit lying there saying, 'I'll just wait until the phone rings. I know he is going to get into trouble.'

"No," I said, "don't say one word to him. But do say this aloud, 'Lord, I surround him with faith.' You see, you have been surrounding him with unbelief."

(Most people do that. They surround their children with unbelief all their lives. I always surrounded mine with faith.)

"Say, 'Lord, I surround him with faith. I do not believe . . . ' Your head won't agree to it; your head will think you are lying, but say, 'I do not agree that he is going to reform school. I do not agree that he is going to wind up in the penitentiary. I do not agree that he is bad. I believe he will be saved. I believe he will turn out right.'

"And keep saying that. Keep saying it until you convince yourself. Oh, you won't believe it at first, because you have been programmed negatively."

Everything in this world is programmed negatively. Newspapers rarely report anything good. It is always bad. Two men killed. Four automobile accidents. A plane crashed. If they do report something such as someone's being appointed or elected to a government office, they always tell what is wrong with them. No one knows anything good about them. They always tell why that person won't make it.

Satan is the god of this world. Satan is a negative god.

Everything in this world is negative.

We are in the world, but we are not of it. Yet even Spirit-filled Christians sit around and soak up all the negative junk on television and in newspapers.

When I was pastoring (before 1949) we didn't have television, but we had radio. One lady in my church stood up and requested prayer for Ma Perkins (the heroine of a daily soap opera). She said, "I think we ought to pray for Ma Perkins. She's going through a trial." She listened to it until she thought it was real. They're always going through a trial on soap operas. Something bad is always happening.

We have to get off that negative side and get over on the positive side!

I said to this woman, "You won't believe it at first. Your head won't let you. But begin to program yourself positively. Keep saying that about your son. If you keep saying it long enough, eventually you will start believing it." I walked off and left her.

Fifteen months later I was back in St. Louis for the FGBMFI convention. When I finished teaching the first session, a lady came running up to the platform.

"Brother Hagin, do you remember me?"

I said, "No, I really don't." I usually remember faces, but she didn't even look familiar.

She said, "Remember, I came up to you last year over at that other hotel wanting you to pray for my boy?"

I said, "Yes, I remember now."

She said, "I was really a little angry with you. I had to repent. God forgave me. But, you know, I did what you said to do. Oh, I want you to know it wasn't easy."

"I didn't tell you it was easy. No fight is easy," I said.

She said, "I had to fight. I had to fight myself—my natural inclinations, my natural mind, my flesh. But I just left that boy alone. I didn't say anything to him about going to church. I didn't nag him. And I had a time. I was used to lying in bed worrying and saying, 'That phone is going to ring any minute. He's in with a gang. He'll get into dope. He is going to the penitentiary.' But, I would just bite my tongue. I would say to myself, 'Don't you say that. You stop that.' Then I would get over on the positive and say, 'No, no, no, I don't believe he is going to reform school. I don't believe he is going to the penitentiary. I believe he will be saved.' I would say that as bravely as I could.

"And then I had to fight the devil. Something would say to me, 'You poor thing. Claiming to be a Christian, and now you've gone to lying. You don't believe that. Can't you see the gang he is running with? You know where he is going to wind up.'

"I had a battle. It took several months before I could really say that and believe it with any conviction. But one Sunday morning he came in at 4 o'clock. I got up to fix a little bite to eat before going to Sunday school and church, and he got up, too. He said, 'Mom, I believe I'll eat breakfast with you.' While we were eating, he said, 'I believe I will go with you this morning.' I hadn't mentioned it for months. I said to him, and I was surprised at myself, 'Now, Son, you didn't get in until 4 o'clock. Maybe you ought to rest and not go.' He said, 'No, I want to go.' I said, 'Are you sure?' He said, 'Yes, I'm going to go.' And we went."

The next week he was out until 4 o'clock on Sunday morning again. But again, he got up and came to the breakfast table. He said, "I'm going to Sunday school and church with you this morning." His mother said, "Son, you were out late. Maybe you ought not go." He said, "No, I want to go." So they went.

Then, on that second Sunday night, he said, "I believe I will go with you tonight." He had been busy running and playing all afternoon. She said, "Son, you have to go to school tomorrow. You probably ought to stay at home and sleep." "No," he said, "I want to go."

He went. And when the altar call was given, without his mother asking him, he marched down front and was saved and filled with the Holy Spirit.

She said to me, "He was 100 percent for the devil before. Now, he is 100 percent for God. He is on fire for God. I want to thank you, Brother Hagin, for putting me on the right track. I've got a brand new boy."

I said, "Praise the Lord!"

She shook hands with me, turned, and walked away two or three steps. Then she turned around and came back. She said, "I want to tell you something else."

I said, "What?"

She said, "He has a brand new momma! I don't worry anymore. I don't worry about anything. Sometimes I almost pinch myself and say, 'Is this really you?' I used to talk so negatively. I was always worrying and talking doubt and unbelief. I was always painting a gloomy picture. But now, I am happy all the time. Praise the Lord! I never worry!"

I said, "I'll tell you something else, Sister, you look so much younger I didn't even recognize you."

Fight the good—not the bad—fight of faith! Caleb and Joshua brought back a good report. Faith always has a good report!

Resist the Devil

Be sure that no doubt or unbelief is permitted in your life concerning the promises of God.

You do not have to doubt.

Somebody said, "Oh, I just can't help it."

Yes, you can. You can if you are a child of God. You can if you have been born again. You see, the man on the inside is a new creature with the Life and Nature of God in it (2 Cor. 5:17). The man who has become a new creature is not the outward man, the body. (If you had brown eyes when you were born again, you still have brown eyes.) But the man on the inside has become a new man. And you do not have to doubt. You can keep from it.

I never have had the problems some people have had. I was saved on the bed of sickness at 16 years of age, and then as a teenager I lived for the Lord. I think one thing that made the difference was, I got into the Word of God on the bed of sickness—I was bedfast 16 months. For the first six months, I couldn't read much. I couldn't see. And because of paralysis I couldn't handle the Bible. After about six months, I got where I could read for an hour at a time. Then after another month or two, I could read about all I wanted.

I got into the Bible. *And I just believed what I read there*. I never doubted it for a moment.

If the Bible said I could do something, I knew I could do it. God would not tell me to do something I could not do. He would be unjust if He did—and He is not unjust.

Yet I've had people everywhere tell me, "I can't do this. I can't do that."

We really ought to throw away the word "can't." You

CAN do anything the Bible says you can do.

If I read where the Bible says, "Believe," I believe that I can believe. I can do what God's Word tells me to do. I am capable, if I am in my right mind, of doing what God's Word says to do. And you are, too.

A woman came up at the close of a service. She said, "Brother Hagin, I want you to pray for me."

I said, "What for?"

"Do I have to tell you?"

I said, "I'm not going to pray unless you do." Then I reminded her that if she expected me to believe with her about something, I have to know what I am believing for. Because I cannot believe beyond the Bible. Faith is based on God's Word.

She tuned up and began to cry, "I'll tell you, Brother Hagin, the cares of life, the burdens of life, and the worries of life are so heavy, I just cannot carry them. I want you to pray that God will do one of two things—that He will either give me grace to bear them, or that He will take about half of them away. I can carry half of them. But I can't carry all of them."

I said, "Sister, I can't pray either prayer. Either prayer would be unscriptural. God doesn't want you to carry even half of them. And God doesn't want to give you the grace to carry all of them. God wants to carry all of them for you.

"Isn't it wonderful," I went on, "that you and I have inside information!" I meant information inside the Word of God. I opened my Bible to First Peter 5:7 and read, *" 'Casting all your care upon him; for he careth for you.'* This tells you exactly what to do about it. Casting ALL your cares on Him—not half of them; not 'pray that God would give you grace'—but, casting ALL your cares on

Him!"

I like the *Amplified* translation of this verse. It is a little more explicit. It says, *"Casting the whole of your care—all your anxieties, all your worries, all your concerns, once and for all—on Him; for he cares for you affectionately, and cares about you watchfully."*

I gave her the Word of God.

She looked at me and said, "Oh, you're hard. You're hard."

I said, "Dear Sister, I didn't write the Bible. It wasn't me who said to cast all of your cares on Him; it was God. He cares for you affectionately and cares about you watchfully. The reason He wants you to cast them on Him is because He loves you. He's not being hard. He loves you. He wants to carry them for you. But He cannot carry them as long as you are carrying them. You have to turn them over to Him. You have to cast them on Him."

She said, "Yes, but you don't know what I've got to worry about."

I said, "I am sure I do not. But I know He does. Let's cast them on Him. Let's turn it over to the Lord."

She said, "Oh, no. I know that I can't. I can't quit worrying."

I said, "That's what the alcoholic says, 'I can't quit drinking.' That's what the cigarette smoker says, 'I can't quit smoking.' That's what the person with the worry habit says, 'I can't quit worrying.' But they can."

Don't use the word "can't." You can. You can do anything the Bible says to do. You can believe. You can refuse to doubt. You can resist the devil and he will flee from you.

The devil is tricky. He puts certain thoughts in your

mind, then he suggests to you, "You must be a terrible person. You couldn't be saved and think those kinds of thoughts." He is constantly endeavoring to get you into doubt and unbelief. If you listen to him, he will do it.

Remember this: *Thoughts may come and persist in staying. But thoughts that are not put into word or action die unborn.*

Remember this also. *The most holy saints of God have found, at times, thoughts in their mind that their heart resented.* Don't listen to your head. Don't let your head dominate you. Let your heart dominate you. Let your spirit dominate you.

Heart Faith

Another thing you should know is this: *Faith will work in your heart with doubt in your head.*

Most Christians are walking by their heads. We contact this world with our mind and with our physical senses. Therefore, whatever is in this world can get into our heads, because we are in contact with this world that way.

Many Christians think they are being honest when they say, "Well, if I said I wasn't doubting I would be lying about it." Just because there is a doubt in your mind, which the devil instilled in one way or another, does not mean you are doubting.

Jesus never said a word about doubt in your head in Mark 11:23. He said, *". . . and shall not doubt in his heart . . . ."*

I know that faith can work in your heart with doubt in your head, because the greatest things that ever happened to me, came even though I had doubt in my head. I just did not pay any attention to my head. I believed in my heart.

When I was healed as a 17-year-old boy of almost total paralysis, a deformed heart, an incurable blood disease, my head was saying all the time, "It will never work." Thoughts were firing to my head faster than a machine gun can fire bullets. "You're not healed. Look at your body. Feel your heart. You're not healed."

I paid no attention to my head. From down on the inside of me I said, "According to the Word of God it is done." Within the hour every symptom disappeared.

It is the same with financial matters. If I had space, I could give you many illustrations. Time after time, my head would say, "It's not working. You don't have the money. Can't you see that you don't have the money? It's not going to work. People are going to find out what a fake you are. This faith business you are preaching won't work. You know it won't work."

I paid no attention to my head. In my heart I said, "It will work because the Word of God said so. I don't care what my head said."

When I lay down at night to go to sleep, my head gave me trouble. Thoughts persisted. "It's not working. Where's the money? Where's the money? You don't have it."

Doubt was in my mind—but I refused to think like that. I got back over into the spirit realm and let my heart dominate me. I said, "According to the Word of God it is done. According to the Word of God it is so. I am going to lie here and praise myself to sleep because the Bible is true. I believe God's Word."

Yes, I know that faith will work in your heart with doubt in your head, because the greatest things that ever happened to me came to pass with doubt in my head. I did not go according to my head. I refused to doubt in my heart.

F. F. Bosworth, a great minister in the first half of this century and author of *Christ the Healer*, said, "If you are going to doubt anything, doubt your doubts. Don't doubt the Word. Don't doubt your faith. Doubt your doubts and believe your beliefs."

The following statement came during an utterance in tongues and interpretation; it registered on my spirit: *Thinking faith thoughts, and speaking faith words, will lead the heart out of defeat and into victory*. Mark that down and don't forget it.

Be sure that no doubt or unbelief is permitted in your life concerning the promises of God.

What are you going to do if they come?

The Bible says, *"Resist the devil, and he will flee from you"* (James 4:7). When you resist doubt, you are resisting the devil. Whatever is of the devil, when you resist that, you are resisting the devil.

If fear comes, speak to it. And fear will come to all of us—fear of disease, fear of failure, fear of a thousand and one things. You can have certain symptoms about your body and the devil will tell you, "You have the beginning of cancer." If you entertain fear, then he will put it on you. Job said, *"For the thing which I greatly feared is come upon me, and that which I was afraid of is come unto me"* (Job 3:25).

One of the greatest fights you will ever have in life is to fight fear. How are you going to do it? With the Word of God. *"Resist the devil, and he will flee from you"* (James 4:7).

The Bible says that God has not given to us the "spirit" of fear:

2 TIMOTHY 1:7
7 For God hath not give us the spirit of fear; but of power, and of love, and of a sound mind.

If God did not give us the spirit of fear—if it did not come from God—there is only one other source, since it is a spirit, it could come from. Therefore, when you resist fear, you are resisting the devil.

Yet people come to me all the time saying (bless their hearts, they don't realize what they are saying, or they wouldn't say it), "Brother Hagin, I resisted and it didn't leave."

"Well," I reply, "God lied, didn't He? He said, 'If you resist the devil he will flee from you.' You resisted him and he didn't flee, so therefore God told a lie."

"Well, no . . . . "

"You just got through saying He did. Because if you resisted the devil and he didn't leave, then the Bible is a lie. If the Bible is a lie, God is a liar. Because the Bible is God's Word. You see, God and His Word are one, just as you and your word are one. If your word is a lie, you are a liar. But why not tell the truth about it? You didn't resist the devil. You made a halfhearted effort. You didn't expect it to work when you started. You are like the woman who prayed about the mountain standing on Mark 11:23, 'Well,' she said, 'Just as I expected; it's still there.' "

Expect! Resist doubt and it will flee from you! Lift your hand and say this out loud:

Faith always has a good report!
I walk by faith;
And not by sight.
I am a faith person.

I refuse doubt.
I refuse fear.
I am a faith child of a faith God.
My faith works.
I always have a good report.
I refuse an evil report.
I am on God's side.
He is on my side.
I belong to God.
I serve God.
I am a child of God.
I believe God.
I believe God that it shall be,
even as it was told me,
in His Holy Word.
God's Word cannot fail.
I cannot fail.
I am standing on the Word.
I am standing on the promises.
Hallelujah!

Step Five: Sincerely desire the benefit you have asked of God.

In Mark 11:24 Jesus said, *"Therefore I say unto you, What things soever ye desire, when ye pray, believe that ye receive them, and ye shall have them."*

There are many important things in this Scripture which need to be emphasized. In this chapter, however, we will focus on the word "desire." It is a very important word. Be sincere about the things you desire.

Many times people have prayed, or requested prayer, and when things did not work out, they said, "I don't know whether or not I really wanted that anyway." That is the reason it did not work.

Another Side

Another side to this, which I will comment on at length, is: You will not be able to push your desire off on

75

somebody else.

We do not say "ye" today. Therefore, we understand it better to read Mark 11:24 like this: " . . . *What things soever* **you** *desire, when* **you** *pray, believe that* **you** *receive them, and* **you** *shall have them.*"

Jesus did not say, "What soever things you desire for your neighbor." You can't always get things for your neighbor unless he wants them. If you could, then you could make your neighbor get saved. God doesn't work that way. If He did, He would make everybody get saved today, and we would all go into the Millennium tomorrow.

God made man and gave him a "choice." Man has a choice and a will of his own. Men are free moral agents. And when you become a Christian, you do not lose that free moral agency.

When another person is involved—that person has to "desire" it, too, for it to work. When another person's will and another person's desires become involved, get them to agree on it. It will not work unless you do.

Agreement

The Bible says, *"Can two walk together, except they be agreed?"* (Amos 3:3). They cannot.

Jesus said, *"Again I say unto you, That if two of you agree on earth as touching any thing that they shall ask, it shall be done for them of my Father which is in heaven"* (Matt. 18:19). Taking the negative side of this verse, He would be saying, "If two of you do not agree, it will not be done." It is really just that simple.

Through the years many people have asked me to pray and agree with them about financial matters, physical needs, etc. I usually join hands with them and say, "You listen to me while I pray. If we both pray at once, you may go one direction and I may go another. There would be no agreement there. So you listen and agree with what I say."

Often I say, "We have just joined hands as an outward physical sign that we are joining our spirits to agree on this thing . . . . " I pray, and agree, and remind the Lord of Matthew 18:19. I count it done—that's what faith does. Then I open my eyes and ask them, "Is it done?"

In many instances, they say, "Brother Hagin, I sure *hope* so."

Immediately, I tell them, "It isn't. There is no agreement. I am *believing* and you are *hoping*. There is no agreement whatsoever."

When two really agree, it works. There is no use in saying, "We agreed and it did not work." That would accuse Jesus Christ of being a liar—and He did not lie. We might as well admit it; we did not agree.

You need not think you are going to push your desire off on somebody else. Each person has a will of his own and desires of his own.

We do desire things for people. We want to help them. And there is a way to help them. We can take them the Word of God. We can get them enlightened with God's Word.

Now it is possible to carry bona fide baby Christians on your faith. You also can carry your own children on your faith when they are small. That is your responsibility. However, when they get older, you cannot continue to carry them. They will have to do it for themselves.

It is the same with husbands and wives. As long as one is a baby Christian, the other can carry that one. But after a while, God will expect that one to do his or her own praying and his or her own believing.

My wife and I were married in November of 1939. Almost a month later, a North-Texas norther blew in. She got a sore throat. She said to me, "The first real cold spell that comes every year, I get a sore throat, and I have it all the winter. I'll have to go to the doctor and get my throat swabbed." (This was the treatment in those days before antibiotics.)

She was a Christian. She had recently been filled with the Holy Spirit. But she had never been taught about faith and healing. Therefore, I knew that in these things she was a spiritual baby and I could carry her. I could make it work for her at this stage of her spiritual development.

So I said, "No, we won't go to the doctor. We won't have your throat swabbed. That chronic throat trouble will leave you and it will never come back."

I did not pray; I just **said** it. I said it based on Mark 11:23. *"Whosoever shall say . . . and shall not doubt in his heart, but shall believe that those things which he saith shall come to pass; he shall have whatsoever he saith."*

The sore throat left and it never has come back.

Ten years later, my wife had some physical problems and the doctor said she needed surgery. I thought she could always ride my faith. But this time I could not make it work. No matter how much I "said" it, she still had all her physical problems. She still needed surgery.

Why didn't it work? Was it because I was not a believer? Was it because my faith did not work?

No. It was because she had had 10 years of spiritual growth. She had sat for 10 years under the teaching of the Word of God. God expected her to learn.

She said about it later, "I had not even tried to develop my faith. I just always thought, *Kenneth will have faith. He will do it.*"

I kept praying about it. I kept trying to get her to believe and not have to have the surgery. I kept trying to get her to the place of healing. But I just could not. She was in pain and misery and suffering. Finally, I said, "All right, I'll tell you what I'll do. I can't get you up to my level of faith. So I will come down to your level and we'll start believing there. What can you believe?"

She said, "I can start out believing that God will see me safely through the operation."

I said, "Okay, I will agree with you."

We found something we could agree on. We agreed that she would come out fine. In fact, I said in my prayer of agreement that she would come through so well the doctors would be astounded.

She had the operation early one morning. About 8 o'clock that night one of the doctors came around and said, "I see by the chart that you haven't had anything for pain."

She said, "That's right."

He said, "Are you hurting? Do you have any pain?"

She said, "No."

He had told me just after the operation that they had made a long incision. I know this may sound a little crude, but this is the way he said it. He said, "Aw, you've got to be hurting, lying up there in bed with your belly cut wide open."

She said, "Well, I don't."

He said, "I'm going to order a shot for you anyway."

That was the only shot they ever gave her.

He said to me afterwards, "I've never seen anything

like this. Nature will heal just so fast. But she has come through this so quickly, it is nothing short of miraculous."

That was not the best miracle God had—but it was still miraculous.

My wife began to exercise her faith. And her faith started growing until she developed strong faith.

Many people expect to ride somebody else's faith all their lives. But they cannot. Some think *I can always ride the pastor's faith.* But they cannot. Then when things don't work, they say, "That faith business doesn't work. I tried it."

That's why it didn't work—they *tried* it. That would be like heading up the highway toward Canada and saying, "I tried to go to Mexico. I couldn't get there. You just can't get to Mexico." It makes just as much sense to say, "I tried that faith business and it doesn't work." Yes, it does work, if you get on the right road and head toward the right direction.

There is something else I want you to see about *agreement* while we are on this. Years ago, I was driving to Kansas City to speak at a Full Gospel Businessmen's convention. I had just finished preaching a six-week meeting in Oklahoma, had driven back to my home in Garland, Texas, and we were going to stop in Tulsa to attend to some business on our way to Kansas City. I had a sense, an inward intuition, of a door flying open and somebody falling out of the car. Usually, when I have these intuitions, I take time to pray and wait on God and find out what it is. (You can pray and avert things.) But because of our busy schedule, I did not take the time.

It was raining, and I thought perhaps it was concerning us. Back then, I didn't wear a seat belt, but on that particular day I put it on. My wife said, "Why did you do that?"

"I don't know," I said. "I keep having an impression of someone being thrown out of the car. I don't know if the Lord is trying to tell us something or not."

We got to Kansas City. During the banquet, before I spoke, someone told me, "You have an emergency long distance phone call." It was our son, Kenneth Hagin Jr. He said that one of my nieces, just 25 years old, had been in an automobile accident.

That's what I had perceived. I wished I had taken time to pray. I am sure I could have averted it.

We got to the hospital in Dallas the next day. The doctors gave her no hope at all. She was conscious. She knew us. We prayed with her. And she began to respond.

In fact, one doctor said to me, almost gleefully, "In her condition, if she just held her own, it would be a miracle. But she is responding. She is improving every hour."

We visited her every day. She was in intensive care, but they would let us in because they realized that when we came in she responded. They would insist that we go in and lay hands upon her and pray and encourage her. Every day she showed improvement. She was coming right along.

Then one morning at 4 o'clock, I suddenly sat straight up in my bed. It seemed as if somebody had touched me. I knew it was the Lord. I said, "Lord, what is it?" I began to search around in my spirit. Then I said, "Ann has quit me."

You see, as long as I could get her to agree with me, I could help her. But I knew on the inside that her spirit had left me. So I said, "Dear Lord, help me to pray about it." I prayed in tongues, then I went back to sleep.

Before I awoke the next morning, the phone was

ringing. Another niece said, "Uncle Ken, come quickly. The doctor wants you to come. Ann is giving up. She wants to die."

The doctors wanted us to come because they said, "Now there really isn't any reason for her dying. But if she wants to, she will."

We rushed to the hospital. She wouldn't even talk to us.

I only know one or two things that happened, but from the evidence of things she said to others, I think she got to praying in the spirit and got so close to the glory world, she looked over there and said, "I would rather be over there than here." She got a peek over there—and she wanted to go home. So she did.

You cannot keep somebody here while they are wanting to go and you are wanting them to stay. We need to clear up some things about *desires* and *agreement*. It's scriptural; it's biblical—but sometimes, folks, it is the easiest thing in the world to die, and the hardest to live. I know; I've been dead twice. Some people just get tired after a while—they would rather go on than stay here. It is not a matter of faith and prayer not working—it is just a matter of their desires, and their will. And you cannot push your desires and your will off on them.

A young minister I knew, a youth minister, was injured in an accident on his part-time job. Somehow there was an open flame always there. He and his brother-in-law, who worked with him, had been warned a number of times by their employer not to handle gasoline around it. But they persisted in doing it. This particular time he had 5 gallons of gasoline in a can with an open top. Some sloshed into the flame, which leaped up to the open can and exploded. Enveloped in flames, he panicked and started to run. His brother-in-law threw him on the ground to roll out the flame.

They rushed him to the hospital. Doctors there would not take the case. He actually became conscious enough in the emergency room to hear them talking. One doctor said, "There is no need to work with him; he will be dead within 45 minutes." Somehow, with his hand lying off the stretcher, he managed to get hold of one doctor's pant leg. He pulled on it and tried to say something. The doctor leaned down and put his ear to the young minister's mouth. He said, "I will live and not die. God will help." This doctor was a Baptist. He said, "If he has that kind of faith, I will take the case."

He kept living. And he made a believer in the infilling of the Holy Spirit with the evidence of speaking in tongues out of that Baptist doctor. When his body would begin to jerk because of nervous shock, he would say, "I've got to pray." Then he would pray in tongues. Since they kept a monitor on him at all times, this would go out over the hospital. Sometimes he would pray and sing in tongues for an hour. His body would quieten. This Baptist doctor said, "I see something. He is in the spirit—and the spirit is dominating the flesh."

He lived for weeks and weeks. But then, I don't know why—perhaps he just got tired—he gave up. This doctor said, "Son, you should have died when they brought you in. We all thought you were going to. But now, there isn't any medical reason why you should die. You are over the crisis. You should live. You made a believer out of me, now don't die and leave us."

But he did—because that is what he desired to do. He told his wife, "I was singing in tongues and I had a vision.

It seemed as if the whole ceiling opened up." He saw the heavenly Jerusalem, and he wanted to go. So he went.

You cannot make somebody else desire what you desire. You cannot push your desires off on somebody else. But, if you can get them to agree with you, great things will happen. When other people's wills and desires are involved, we have to work on getting them to agree with us.

Choice

If we could push our desires off on others, God would push His desires off on us. But He gives us His Word. He gives us the *choice* to walk in the Word or reject it.

Some extreme teaching says, "God is all-powerful. God can do anything He wants to do. If He wants to, He just knocks heads together and does it, no matter what."

I was preaching in a church in North Texas and I said, "Some people think God can do anything He wants to, whenever He wants to, wherever He wants to, under any kind of circumstances."

A fellow on the second pew from the front spoke right out loud and said, "Bless God, I do."

I didn't know him. The pastor didn't know him. He just happened to come to the meeting that night. But when he blurted that out, without thinking—I know the Spirit of God inspired me—I said, "Well, if He can, why doesn't He make you pay your tithes?"

He ducked down behind the solid wooden pew so I couldn't see him.

God gives us His Word. He tells us about paying tithes. He tells us about giving offerings. He tells us the blessings and benefits of it. He allows us to use our own wills and make our own choices about it.

One man was so thrilled as he told me about the "new revelation" someone had just preached in their church. It went like this: God is all-powerful. Yes. God can do anything He wants to do. Yes. God is not willing that any should perish. Yes. Therefore, nobody is going to perish; everybody is going to be saved.

NO! Jesus said, *"Go ye into all the world, and preach the gospel to every creature. He that believeth and is baptized shall be saved; but he that believeth not shall be damned"* (Mark 16:15,16).

God made man and gave him a choice—a will of his own. God planned a wonderful plan of redemption. Jesus consummated that plan. But man must choose to accept what God has provided.

Too many times people run to the excess. After their uncle died, some people asked me about it. "Brother Hagin, we all prayed. We believed God. We claimed his healing for him. But he died."

"What did he claim?" I asked them.

"Well, he said all the time that he was going to die."

I said, "He got what he said."

Jesus plainly said, *" . . . he shall have whatsoever he saith"* (Mark 11:23). He did not say, "He shall have whatsoever you say for him." Certainly their prayer of faith would work as far as God is concerned. But right on the other hand, that man had a will. That man could choose.

We cannot dominate one another's wills. You are not going to get somebody healed while they are believing they are going to die, and you are believing they are going to live. There is no agreement there. You have to go to work on them and talk them out of dying and into living.

I remember one outstanding case. The first week I went to pastor one church, I was asked to visit a dear 82-year-old woman who was in the hospital suffering from cancer of the stomach. The doctors said she had 10 days to live.

I did not pray for healing the first time I went to visit her. In fact, it was a long time before I did. She wasn't ready to accept it. I began to talk to her about healing. I read her Scriptures on the subject.

She said, "Brother Hagin, I'm 82 years old. I've lived my life out. I'm saved and filled with the Holy Spirit. Just let me go. I've suffered so. Just leave me alone and let me die."

I said, "I'm not going to do it. Let God heal you, Grandma, and then die if you want to. But don't die like this. God won't get any glory out of this."

You see, I had to talk her out of dying first before I could get her healed. There was no use in praying that God would heal her—really, as far as He was concerned, He had already done it. So I just knelt by her bed and prayed, "Dear God, help Grandma not to cast away her confidence."

Then I stayed firm and visited her two or three times a week. I just kept putting Scriptures into her. I kept talking her out of dying. Finally I got her talked out of dying, and into living. She was instantly healed. She jumped up and started dancing like a 16-year-old. The cancer disappeared. She could eat anything she wanted. And she lived to be 94 before she died without sickness and disease and went home to be with Jesus.

Short Summation

When it comes to you as an individual, remember this: Sincerely desire the benefit you asked of God. Then know that God's Word works. *"What things soever you desire, when you pray, believe that you receive them, and you shall have them."*

When other people's wills and desires are involved, you will have to work on getting them to agree with you.

Step Six: Ask God in faith, nothing wavering, believing that what is asked is yours.

Do not take these steps out of their setting. They are to be taken in order. Suppose there are ten steps leading up to a platform. You may get into difficulty trying to step from the bottom to the top. But if you take one step at a time, it is easy.

At this point I am assuming you have already taken Steps One through Five. Now we come to Step Six: *Ask God in faith, nothing wavering, believing that what is asked is yours*. You are ready now to pray and receive what you desire from God.

Kinds of Prayer

Let me make an important observation. The church world as a whole has missed it in the prayer business and in the prayer life. And this is where we have missed it: We have put all prayer in the same sack and shook it all out together. We said, in effect, "Prayer is prayer." We failed to realize that the New Testament teaches there are different kinds of prayer. And different rules apply to different kinds of praying. The same rules will not apply to all kinds of praying.

I use sports as an illustration. In the realm of sports there is football; there is baseball; there is golf; there is tennis. All are sports. But they are not all played by the same rules. It would be foolish to say, "Sports are sports. All sports ought to be played by football rules."

It would make just as much sense to say, "Prayer is prayer. All prayer ought to be prayed by the same rules." That would be stupid. But that is where we have missed it.

For instance, when you pray a "prayer of dedication and consecration," you do not use the same rules you use when you pray a "prayer to receive something from God."

When I pray a "prayer of consecration and dedication," I am not necessarily praying to receive something from God. I am dedicating myself to do whatever God wants me to do. I say, "God, *if* You want me to go to Africa, I will go." That means I don't know whether He wants me to go or not. But *if* He wants me to go, I am available. So I can put an "if" in that prayer.

When I pray a "prayer to receive something from God," I cannot put an "if" in it and ever get an answer. In this kind of prayer "if" indicates unbelief—"if" is the badge of doubt.

In the "prayer of consecration and dedication," I can put an "if." "*If* You want me to stay home, I will stay home. *If* You want me to go preach, I will go preach. Whatever You want me to do, I will do. *If* You want me to go talk to that person about being saved, I will do it."

There is another kind of prayer where we are not asking for anything, not trying to change anything; we are just worshipping God. This is the "prayer of worship." Different rules apply to this prayer.

I do not have space to go into all the different kinds of praying and the rules that apply. (I do have books on the subject and I teach it in detail every winter in our annual Winter Bible Seminar.) But I am making these brief observations about the different kinds of prayer here, so that you will understand I am talking about one kind of praying here in Step Six. And that is: "The prayer to receive something from God."

MARK 11:24
24 Therefore I say unto you, What things soever ye desire, when ye pray, believe that ye receive them, and ye shall have them.

In this verse, Jesus is talking about praying to receive *things* from God. *"What **things** soever ye desire . . . ."* Do not take it out of context. He is talking about believing and receiving. He gives explicit instructions.

What are the rules that apply?

". . . when ye pray . . . ." After you pray? No. When it comes to pass? No. The moment you pray—**believe!**

Believe what?

"I believe in God." That's wonderful—but it won't work here.

"I believe in the baptism in the Holy Spirit and speaking in tongues." That's wonderful—but it won't work here.

"I believe the Bible is true." That's fine—but it won't

work here."

"I believe Jesus is the Son of God." That's right and good—but it won't work here."

What is it you are supposed to believe?

". . . believe that ye receive them . . . ." Believe that you receive *them*—the *things* you were praying for.

"Yes," somebody might say, "but I don't have them yet."

I know it. If you had them, you wouldn't have to believe it. You would know it.

"Well, I'm not going to believe I've got something my physical senses don't tell me I have."

You will have to do without it then, because you will never get it. It is just that simple.

Nothing Wavering

JAMES 1:5-7
5   If any of you lack wisdom, let him ask of God, that giveth to all men liberally, and upbraideth not; and it shall be given him.
6   But let him ask in faith, nothing wavering. For he that wavereth is like a wave of the sea driven with the wind and tossed.
7   For let not that man think that he shall receive any thing (wisdom or anything else) of the Lord.

James is writing about receiving. He is writing to Christians. Yet he tells some of them, in effect, "There is no use in thinking you are going to get anything, because you are not. Not because God doesn't want to give it to you, but because you are wavering."

Wavering. He that wavereth is like the wave of the sea,

dashed about by the wind and driven.

Stand your ground and do not waver. Ask of God in faith, nothing wavering, believing that what is asked is yours.

Step Seven: Do not tolerate for one single moment a thought to the contrary but that it is yours.

2 CORINTHIANS 10:5
5 Casting down imaginations, and every high thing that exalteth itself against the knowledge of God, and bringing into captivity every thought to the obedience of Christ.

Let every thought and desire affirm that you have what you asked in prayer. Never permit a mental picture of failure to remain in your mind. Never doubt for one minute that you have the answer. If doubts persist, rebuke them. The Bible says to resist the devil, and he will flee from you (James 4:7). Doubt is the devil. Resist doubts and rebuke them. Get your mind on the answer.

Eradicate every image, suggestion, vision, dream, impression, feeling, and all thoughts that do not contribute to your faith that you have what you ask. To eradicate means to uproot or remove.

The devil can move in the suggestion realm. Some people think that every feeling, vision, dream, or impression they have is from God, but Satan can move in that realm as well. You have to be able to know whether it is God or the devil. Those things that do not contribute to your faith are of the devil. Eradicate them.

A minister friend of mine had built up a notable church which he had founded and pastored for 25 years. Then at the age of 50, he was going to have to quit his work because of a physical deficiency. He was a Full Gospel minister, but he did not believe for his healing.

This was because as he awoke one morning he saw someone in his room in shining apparel. He thought it was Jesus. This person said, "It is not my will to heal you."

It could not have been Jesus. Matthew 8:17 says, "... *Himself took our infirmities, and bare our sicknesses.*" Jesus is the Word of God. Jesus is God speaking to us. If you want to see God at work, look at Jesus. He went about doing good and healing all that were oppressed of the devil (Acts 10:38).

If Jesus appeared to you in a vision and said that it was not His will to heal you, He would be making Himself out to be a liar. Could it be His will for you not to have what He bore for you?

No! It was the devil that brought that vision to my minister friend—and he accepted it. God does not propagate doubt and unbelief. Every suggestion, vision, image, dream, impression, and all thoughts that do not contribute to your faith that you have what you ask should be completely destroyed.

Thoughts are governed by observation, association, and teachings. Guard against every evil thought that comes into the mind. Stay away from all places and things that do not support your affirmation that God has answered prayer. You may even have to stay away from some churches—those that put out more unbelief than anything else.

We have talked about what not to think on—now let's see from the Word of God exactly what you are to think on:

Finally, brethren,
whatsoever things are true,
whatsoever things are honest,
whatsoever things are just,
whatsoever things are pure,
whatsoever things are lovely,
whatsoever things are of good report;
if there be any virtue,
and if there be any praise,
think on these things.

—Philippians 4:8

Step Eight: Count the thing done that you have asked.

Here is the thing that divides the men from the boys. I have been teaching faith in God's Word for more than 60 years. I know it works. I have proved it in my own life. But I know from experience that some of the things I teach bother some people. I do not teach them to be controversial. I prove everything I say by the Scripture. I do not teach what I think. I teach what I know. Then I let people do their own thinking.

There are two main areas where I get the most dissent. I do not have space to get into one of them—but one of the main objections is right here: *Calling those things which be not as though they were.* Yet I can prove from the Bible that is exactly what faith does.

A Type of Our Faith

The faith of Abraham is a type of our faith. The New

99

Testament speaks of Abraham as the *"father of all them that believe . . . who also walk in the steps of that faith of our father Abraham . . . . "* (Rom. 4:11,12).

GALATIANS 3:29
29 And if ye be Christ's, then are ye Abraham's seed, and heirs according to the promise.

Are you Christ's? Then you are Abraham's seed—not the physical seed, but the spiritual seed, the faith seed.

GALATIANS 3:7
7 Know ye therefore that they which are of faith, the same are the children of Abraham.

We are the faith children of Abraham because we have the same kind of faith he had. What kind of faith did he have? He called those things that be not as though they were.

ROMANS 4:17
17 (As it is written, I have made thee a father of many nations,) before him whom he believed, even God, who quickeneth the dead, and calleth those things which be not as though they were.

Somebody said, "Yes, but that's talking about God there, who calls those things which be not as though they were."

First, if it is wrong for me to call things which be not as though they were, it is wrong for God to do it.

Second, why does God call those things that be not as though they were? Because He is a faith God.

Third, we are faith children of a faith God. Therefore, we ought to act like God and call those things which be not as though they were. Children of the devil act like the devil. Children of God ought to act like God (Eph. 5:1). One way God acts is, He calls those things which be not as though they were.

Fourth, in the Cambridge Bible, the marginal reference to *"before him"* reveals that the Greek reads, *"like unto him."* In other words, Abraham did just like God did. He called those things which be not as though they were — and that was his faith.

A Personal Experience

Looking back now over my own life, I can see clearly how certain things worked—even though at the time I did not see things in the light I see them now. Yet I was led of the Spirit, and the Spirit always leads us in line with the Word of God.

Soon after I was healed and raised from a bed of sickness, and after I'd entered the ministry, I awoke one Monday morning with the right side of my face paralyzed. It was numb. I could pinch it, slap it, and not feel anything. It would not move. When I talked, the left side of my mouth took all the movement. When I laughed, the left corner of my mouth seemed to run all the way around to my ear.

As I lay down to go to sleep Monday night, I realized even more was involved. One eye would not shut. (Have you ever tried to go to sleep with one eye shut and one eye open? It's not easy.) I reached up with my finger and pulled the eyelid down carefully. It slowly opened back up.

But I had already said, "I know what I will do. (I was a Baptist boy. But I had learned about healing and had been healed by the power of God reading Grandma's Methodist

Bible.) I will go down to the Full Gospel Tabernacle Wednesday night and have Brother Conner anoint me with oil and pray. And I will be healed."

I got into the service a little late and sat in the back of the crowd of about 300. I usually attended their Wednesday night services, so I knew they would testify, pray, have a Bible lesson, and wind up by gathering around the altar to pray. This night, however, they had attended to some extra business and Brother Conner said, "Because of the lateness of the hour, we will just stand and offer the benediction."

They were about to go, so I lifted my hand and shouted from the back of the room, "Brother Pastor, I want you to pray for my healing, please."

"All right," he said, "come right on."

I marched down that old sawdust aisle and stood before the pulpit, while he anointed my forehead with oil, laid his hand upon my head, and prayed.

I don't know till this day one word he said. I was waiting to hear that word, "Amen." At that time I did not realize why. Now I know that was my "point of contact"— the point where I was going to start "believing I receive" my healing.

Here is a crucial point concerning the prayer of faith: It "believes I receive it" before I have it (Mark 11:24). It calls those things which be not as though they were (Rom. 4:17).

When I heard Brother Connor say, "Amen," in faith I lifted my hand and shouted, "Thank God, it's gone!"

Even as I said that, one corner of my mouth pulled almost around to my ear. I had no physical evidence, no feeling of healing.

"Well," someone might say, "you lied about it."

No, I did not. *I was calling those things which be not as though they were.* I think there is nothing spoken in the Bible which is quite so hard for most Christians to do.

Many honest people think they would be lying if they did, and they fear to do it. But think for a moment. Consider these facts. The Bible says that God cannot lie (Heb. 6:18). He is Truth and cannot lie. And Romans 4:17 says that God, who cannot lie, calls those things which be not as though they were. If, when God calls those things which be not as though they were, He is not lying—then when I call those things which be not as though they were, I am not lying.

Revelation 13:8 tells us God called Jesus as a Lamb slain from the foundation of the world—thousands of years before it happened.

Ephesians 1:4 says we were chosen in Christ before the foundation of the world—and we were not even born yet.

The Bible says that God told Abraham, *"I have made thee a father of many nations"* (Gen. 17:5; Rom. 4:17). He did not say, "I am going to do it." Abraham and Sarah had no children—and none in sight. He was 100 and she was 90. It was naturally impossible. But God did not say, "I am going to do it." God calleth those things which be not as though they were. He said, "I have done it."

And Abraham believed LIKE UNTO GOD! He called those things which be not as though they were.

When Christians can be persuaded to take that step of faith—they will get results!

When I shouted after Brother Conner prayed, "Thank God, it's gone," I was being LIKE UNTO HIM and calling those things which be not as though they were.

Brother Conner said, "That's just like Jesus," and

asked me to give the benediction.

People rushed up and said, "Did the Lord really heal you, Kenneth?"

"He surely did."

"Your face still looks twisted. Do you feel any different?"

"Not that I can tell."

"You don't look any different, and you say you don't feel any different. What makes you think the Lord healed you?"

I said, "I don't think it; I know it."

"What makes you say that?"

"The Word makes me say it. The Word says I am healed—and I believe it."

(I am using healing as an illustration, but the principles of faith are so in any realm—spiritual, physical, material. Concerning financial needs, for instance, I learned to call those things which be not as though they were—and they became! **Faith calleth those things which be not as though they were!** I wish I could shout that from every housetop in the world.)

Several young couples walked home together from that Wednesday night service. "Kenneth, did the Lord really heal you?" they persisted.

"He surely did."

"We noticed when we passed under the street light that when you laughed, one side of your mouth moved, and the other side did not. What makes you think you are healed?"

"I don't think it; I know it."

"We don't understand it."

"I don't understand it either," I said, "but Jesus did not say, 'Therefore whatsoever things you desire, when you pray, *if you understand it*, you will have them.' "

No, Jesus said, "Believe that you receive them, and you will have them."

Soon the other couples went in their directions and I walked the young lady I was with to her door. She invited me inside and called her mother to the front of the house. Maneuvering me under a light, she said, "Momma, I want you to look at Kenneth's face."

She and her mother were short women. I couldn't keep from laughing as they stared up intently into my face. When I did, my face twisted.

"I feel silly," her mother said. "What am I looking for?"

"Does Kenneth's face look any different than it did before we went to church?"

"Not that I can tell. Why?"

"Well, he thinks he's healed."

"Imogene," I said, "I don't *think* I'm healed; I *know* I'm healed."

You see, I was calling those things which be not as though they were. I was acting like God. He wants us to act like Him. If it is a sin to do that, then God is the biggest sinner in the universe. He has been doing it for thousands of years. No! It is not a sin to act upon God's Word. It is being *humble*. We humble ourselves and walk in the light of God's Word.

We are to walk by faith and not by sight (2 Cor. 5:7). Sight never calls those things which be not as though they were. Walking by sight is to walk by reason. Reason never calls those things which be not as though they were. Sight walks by what it sees. Sight walks by what the physical senses tell it. It says, "If I see it, if I feel it, then I will believe I have it."

That does not please God. It displeases Him (Heb.

11:6). It is not faith.

HEBREWS 11:1
1 Now faith is the substance of things hoped for,
the evidence of things not seen.

Faith is the substance, the ground, the confidence, of *things* hoped for. It is the evidence of *things* not seen.

Many times during the past 60 years I have gone right on with physical symptoms in my body which belied my testimony. The devil would say to my mind, "You're lying." But I said to the devil, "My faith is giving substance . . . . My faith is giving substance to the things not seen. No, I don't see the healing, and I don't feel it. But my faith is giving substance to it." As I continued to make that confession and to praise God, it became *substance!*

The moment prayer is made should be the moment you begin to call those things which be not as though they were. Even though, in the case of healing, the disease may seem to progress and grow worse. **Hold fast to your confession of faith—calling those things which be not as though they were!**

That night many years ago, my young lady friend said, "Brother Conner didn't pray the prayer of faith. That's where the trouble is."

The very fact that Brother Conner anointed me with oil, and that his church kept a bottle of oil on the pulpit, showed they believed in James 5:14. That's why, as a Baptist, I had gone there rather than to my church.

In the final analysis, you see, it is my faith which determines the extent of my blessing. Jesus said to two blind men, "Believe ye that I am able to do this?" When they answered, "Yea, Lord," He touched their eyes and said,

"According to your faith be it unto you" (Matt. 9:27-29).

I told Imogene, "I am healed by faith, and the next time you see me, you will admit it is so yourself." I knew the manifestation had to be forthcoming.

That night, as I lay in bed, one eye was shut and one was open. The devil said, "You're not healed. And now you've made a fool of yourself before everybody."

I said, "Mr. Devil, I'm just going to lie right here and praise myself to sleep."

It was past midnight. So I began to praise the Lord saying, "I want to thank you, Lord, because last night I was healed."

When I awoke the next morning, my face was just as straight as it is now. After breakfast I went over to Imogene's house. I smiled at her, with my face straight.

"Well," she said, "I see you got your healing."

"Yes," I said, "last night when Brother Conner anointed me and prayed."

"You weren't healed when you left here," she insisted.

(If I had been trying to get healed on her faith, it never would have materialized. She believed it when she saw it.)

Confession

Some folks, bless their hearts, would never say the things they say if they read the Bible. But, you see, they are not in the Bible—they are not in the spirit—they are in natural human reasoning. Some people call it the sense knowledge realm.

Some say, "There's nothing to that confession business."

If there isn't—there is nothing to salvation.

Stop and think about it—that's how you got saved. The Bible says, " . . . *with the mouth confession is made unto salvation.*"

ROMANS 10:9,10
9 That if thou shalt CONFESS WITH THY MOUTH the Lord Jesus (or, Jesus as Lord), and shalt believe in thine heart that God hath raised him from the dead, thou shalt be saved.
10 For with the heart man believeth unto right-eousness; and WITH THE MOUTH CONFESSION is made unto salvation.

Righteousness here means right standing with God. No one can make himself right with God. Jesus—through His death, burial, and resurrection—made us right with God. A person believes that in his heart—because the Bible tells him about it. Then, with the mouth—with what?—with the *mouth* confession is made unto salvation.

You could read Romans 10:10 like this: "With the heart man believes he is right with God because Jesus died, took his sins, was made sin for him, was raised from the dead. With the mouth man confesses he is saved."

A person must confess he is saved before it ever happens. If he did not, faith would have no part in it. It is his confession that brings it into being.

The new birth is based on faith. It is based on confession. Anybody who knows the Bible at all knows that. But too many Christians want to stop right there. We need to realize that *anything* we get from God comes the same way.

God is a faith God. We are faith children. It is always with the heart that man believes, and with the mouth that confession is made unto—not only unto the new birth, but unto divine healing, unto the baptism in the Holy Spirit, unto answers to prayer.

Pleasing God

HEBREWS 11:6
6 But without faith it is impossible to please him; for he that cometh to God must believe that he is, and that he is a rewarder of them that diligently seek him.

Sin is disobeying God.

Holiness is simply obeying and pleasing God in all things at all times. One part of God's will—and people want to be in the will of God—is that we call those things which be not as though they were. This attitude honors God, because we are believing His Word without outward evidence. That pleases Him. It puts us into an attitude of faith to receive great things from God.

The vast majority of Christians who testify, "I want my life to please the Lord" are thinking about right conduct and good works. The Bible teaches right conduct and good works—but you can have right conduct and good works and still not please God.

Nowhere does the Bible say, "Without right conduct and good works it is impossible to please God." He did not put the emphasis there. He did say, *"Without **faith** it is impossible to please Him."*

Smith Wigglesworth said, "There is something about believing God that will cause Him to pass over a million people just to get to you."

Count the thing done that you have asked. Follow in the steps of that faith of our father Abraham, who followed in the steps of the faith of God. Call those things that be not as though they were!

Step Nine: Give glory to God even before it comes into manifestation.

You have counted it done (Step 8), but it has not yet come into manifestation.

Let's look further at the faith of Abraham—in whose faith steps we are to follow—for a Scripture on which to base Step Nine.

> **ROMANS 4:19-21**
> **19 And being NOT WEAK in faith, he considered not his own body now dead, when he was about an hundred years old, neither yet the deadness of Sarah's womb:**
> **20 He staggered not at the promise of God through unbelief; but was STRONG in faith, GIVING GLORY TO GOD;**
> **21 AND BEING FULLY PERSUADED that, what he had promised, he was able also to perform.**

What did Abraham do?

He gave glory to God!

What did he give glory to God for?

He was fully persuaded that what God had promised, He was able also to perform!

You see, He had not yet performed it. It had not yet come to pass. But Abraham counted it as done, and was giving glory to God—*before it was manifested*—because he believed that what God had promised He was able to perform.

Did you notice verse 20 calls that *strong* faith?

It says Abraham was *strong* in faith *"giving glory to God and being fully persuaded."* That's what the Bible calls *strong* faith.

Are you fully persuaded that what God has promised He is able to perform? That whatever He has promised in His Word He can do? If your answer is yes, then you are half-strong in faith. That is half of it.

The second half requires a yes answer to this question: Can you give glory to God? Can you praise God? Can you say, "Thank You, Father, for Your promise"? If your answer is yes again, then you are strong in faith.

In your waking moments, think on the greatness of God and His goodness. Count your blessings. Lift your heart to God constantly in gratitude and increasing praise for what He has done and for what He is doing for you now.

PHILIPPIANS 4:6
6 Be careful for nothing; but in every thing by prayer and supplication WITH THANKSGIVING let your requests be made known unto God.

The phrase "be careful for nothing" means "in nothing

be anxious." The *Amplified* translation reads, "Do not fret or have any anxiety about anything." As long as you are fretful and anxious, praying and fasting will do no good.

This Scripture says, *"with thanksgiving"*—and this comes after praying about it. You thank Him for it after you have prayed for it.

Make every prayer relative to what you have asked a statement of faith instead of unbelief. You can say that you do have faith as easily as you can think thoughts of doubt and unbelief. It is thinking faith thoughts and speaking faith words that leads the heart out of defeat and into victory.

Do not accept defeat. Do not be denied. It is your family right, your redemptive right, to have what God has promised. It is yours now, so accept it and it will become a reality.

Smith Wigglesworth said, "If you pray seven times for any one thing, you prayed six times in unbelief."

Andrew Murray said, "It is not good taste to ask God for the same thing over and over again. If, when you do pray again, what you have prayed for has not materialized, don't pray for it again in the same way. That would be unbelief. Remind God that you asked for it and what His Word says, and tell Him that you are expecting it. Then thank Him for it."

Many people undo their prayers. They get into unbelief and stay there, spinning their wheels.

I am convinced that if most Christians would quit praying and start praising God, the answer would materialize right away.

Step Ten: Act as though you have received what you asked.

There is always some way in which you can act.

When I was bedfast as a teenager more than 55 years ago, I say that truth. I asked myself the question, "What would I do if I were up from here?"

I answered, "I would preach; that's what I would do."

So I began to get ready to preach, even though at that time I was in a partially paralyzed condition. I began to put together sermon notes until I finally had a whole box of them. Only one of them was preachable, but I was acting like it was true.

There is always some way you can act—not in presumption, but in faith.

In Summation

I want to wrap up some things as we conclude.

Remember that the moment you wonder why God has not answered, or you look around for some reason why He did not hear your prayer, or you begin to accept the delay in the answer as the will of God for you not to have what you have asked, *you are defeated.*

You are automatically defeated because you failed to hold firm in unwavering faith in God for the answer.

Remember that Step Two was: *Find Scriptures that promise you the things you ask for and are believing for.* If the Bible says it, we are to believe it.

"Well," someone might say, "it might not be God's will for me to have that."

If it is not God's will for us to have it, then God lied. Unconsciously, many Christians accuse God of being a liar. If they knew what they were doing, they would not do it.

You see, if God promises you something in His Word, or

in His Word He tells you something belongs to you, *He intends for you to have it!* If He does not, then He is fooling you and He is a partner to trickery. But He is not a partner to trickery.

In spiritual things, if people would just fight for what belongs to them like they do in the natural, it would solve a lot of difficulties.

In the natural if somebody came by and said, "You are going to have to move out of this house," and you had been living there 25 years and had it paid for, you would say, "This is mine. Here is the piece of paper that says it is mine."

You would not say, "Well, give me 10 days and I will move out and give it to you." No, you would get a lawyer if necessary. You have the legal document that says it is yours.

God's Word is a legal document. The New Testament (testament means will) is the will of God for me to have everything His Word says is mine. And I am not going to lie down, play dead, and give in to the devil. I am going to have what God says I can have.

You can, too! But you cannot waver about it.

Never, under any circumstances, question the will of God in the matter of unanswered prayer, since He has promised that you can have whatsoever you ask if you do not doubt.

Jesus said, *"What things soever* (that's a broad ticket!) *ye desire, when ye pray, believe that ye receive them, and ye shall have them"* (Mark 11:24).

A lot of people say, "Yes, but . . . . "

There's not a "but" in there—so don't add one!

"Yes, but that means this . . . . "

No, if Jesus did not mean what He said, then He lied about it. It is just that simple. If Jesus did not mean what He said, He told a lie about it and He is hypocritical.

I do not believe the Son of God is a liar. I do not believe He is hypocritical. I believe He told the truth.

Whether or not your prayer is answered depends on you more than it does on God.

God has already made certain promises and certain statements. The Bible says, God never fails, God does not change, God cannot lie. Then, if He promises you the things you are praying about, He is not going to change and say, "No, you can't have it." He cannot lie. Therefore, if you do not get it, it depends upon you more than it does upon God.

Most people misinterpret John 15:7 as if it read like this: "If ye abide in me, and my words abide in you, ye shall ask whatever God wills, and it shall be done unto you, if it is the will of God."

Is that what it says?

No. It reads like this:

JOHN 15:7
7 If ye abide in me, and my words abide in you, ye shall ask what ye will, and it shall be done unto you.

What Ye will! What YOU will!

As an individual, since August of 1934, I never prayed about one single thing without getting it.

Not one time did God ever say, "No." Not one time did He say, "Wait a while." All such reasoning as that is human reasoning. The Bible does not teach that.

What are the conditions in John 15:7?

First, you abide in Him. In other words, you are born

again and in Him.

Second, His Words abide in you. This is why Step 2 in our series is, "Find the Scriptures . . . . " Abide in the Word. Let His Words abide in you.

Many times—even though I know the Scriptures, even though I can quote them—I do not pray about some things immediately. I go back to the Word. I go over those Scriptures which apply carefully—sometimes for a day or two—before I ever pray. For, not only must I abide in Him, but His Word must abide in me. Then I shall ask what I will and it shall be done unto me.

Do not make the mistake multiplied thousands of Christians are making. That is, wondering and wavering concerning the will of God in anything that is promised by God. Remember what the Spirit of God said through the Apostle James (James 1:5-7). The person who doubts or wavers is not to think he or she shall receive *anything* of the Lord.

Too many Christians are praying in the dark. They are not praying in the light of God's Word. They have not found the Scriptures which promise them the thing they are praying for (Step 2). They are not praying in the light which the entrance of His Word gives (Ps. 119:130).

A husband and wife came for the wife's healing at the end of one service. Her case was incurable. Doctors had said she would be dead within six months.

"We have been praying that if it is the will of God to heal her, He will give us faith so she can be healed," the husband said.

"How are you going to know whether it is the will of God to heal her or not?" I asked.

"Well, we thought that you would lay hands on her, and if it is God's will, He would heal her, and if it is not, He wouldn't."

I said, "No, I refuse to pray under those circumstances, because she will not be healed. Then you would go off and say it is not the will of God—and you would be further away from it instead of closer to it."

(Many people are in worse shape after prayer than they were in before prayer. They ought not to have been prayed for in certain instances.)

The husband looked at me blankly and asked, "What am I to do?"

I said, bringing him back to the Word, "Now I am not saying that it says it (of course, I knew it did), but if the Word of God said that Jesus took your wife's infirmities and bare her sicknesses, would it be God's will to heal her?"

He said, "Certainly."

"Well," I said, "let's find out whether it says it or not." I took them to Matthew 8:17, Isaiah 53:4 and 5, and First Peter 2:24.

They saw it. The husband said, "You know, the first part of our prayer wasn't any good. We're going to have to throw it away, aren't we?"

I didn't tell him right then, but they had to throw away their entire prayer before they could get results.

Their prayer had been that if it was God's will to heal her, He would give them faith to receive the healing. And they were going to ascertain whether or not it was God's will to heal her by whether or not she was healed when I laid hands on her.

That's not the way you find out the will of God. You find out the will of God by going to the will of God.

We know about the last will and testament of someone

who has died. Well, we have the New Testament—the will of God—secured to us, the Church, by the blood and death of our Lord Jesus Christ. Read the will and find out what belongs to you!

"We are going to have to throw that first part of our prayer away," the husband said. "All we have to do now is pray that God will give us faith so that she can be healed."

"No," I said, "we can't pray yet. We're not ready yet. Are you saved?"

"We are members of _____ Church."

"You could be a member of this church where we're holding this meeting and not be saved. Have you been born again? Are you a child of God?"

"Oh, yes."

"How did you get saved?"

"Our neighbors kept inviting us to go to church with them, and finally we did. When the minister gave the invitation, we went forward and knelt at the altar. He laid hands on our heads and prayed, and he encouraged us to pray."

"Did you pray that God would give you faith so you could be saved?" I asked.

"Oh, no. The minister had just preached that Christ died for our sins according to the Scriptures. He had preached that whosoever shall call upon the Name of the Lord shall be saved. We knew what the Lord would do before we went down there."

"Well," I said, "He not only bore your sins, but He bore your sicknesses. So why pray that God would give you faith so you could be healed? All you have to know is what God's Word says."

He jumped up and said, "We're going to have to throw

away that whole prayer, aren't we?"

We were ready for prayer then. He knew the will of God. She knew the will of God. To make a long story short, the woman received her healing. I saw them years later and she still was well.

Let me say it one more time: In the final analysis the answer to your prayer depends upon you more than it does upon God. This is true for the simple reason that God does not fail, God does not change, God does not lie, and there is no possibility of a failure on His part. The only failure possible is on man's part.

Man is accustomed to living by feelings instead of by faith. But the Bible says that we walk by faith and not by sight (2 Cor. 5:7). "Sight" encompasses any of the physical senses or feelings. We do not walk by that. We walk by faith. We live by faith. But man is so used to walking by feelings instead of faith, so used to being swayed by circumstances instead of calling those things which be not as though they were, that he simply does not doggedly hold to the right steps. And that is what defeats him. That is where the failure is.

You must see to it that YOU do not fail. Then, because God does not fail, there cannot be a faint possibility of a prayer failure or a faith failure in your life.

ABOUT THE AUTHOR

The ministry of Kenneth E. Hagin has spanned more than 65 years since God miraculously healed him of a deformed heart and incurable blood disease at the age of 17. Today the scope of Kenneth Hagin Ministries is worldwide. The ministry's radio program, "Faith Seminar of the Air," is heard on more than 300 stations nationwide and on the Internet worldwide. Other outreaches include: *The Word of Faith*, a free monthly magazine; crusades, conducted nationwide; RHEMA Correspondence Bible School; RHEMA Bible Training Center; RHEMA Alumni Association and RHEMA Ministerial Association International; and a prison ministry.

The Word of Faith is a full-color magazine
with faith-building teaching articles by
Rev. Kenneth E. Hagin and Rev. Kenneth Hagin Jr.

The Word of Faith also includes encouraging true-life
stories of Christians overcoming circumstances
through God's Word, and information on the
various outreaches of Kenneth Hagin Ministries
and RHEMA Bible Church.

To receive a free subscription to The Word of Faith, call:
1-888-28-FAITH
(1-888-283-2484)
www.rhema.org

RHEMA
Bible Training Center

Want to reach the height of your potential?

RHEMA can take you there.

| proven instructors
| alumni benefits
| career placement
| hands-on experience
| curriculum you can use

Do you desire —

- to find and effectively fulfill God's plan for your life?
- to know how to "rightly divide the Word of truth"?
- to learn how to follow and flow with the Spirit of God?
- to run your God-given race with excellence and integrity?
- to become not only a laborer but a *skilled* laborer?

If so, then RHEMA Bible Training Center is here for you!

For a free video and full-color catalog, call:

1-888-28-FAITH
(1-888-283-2484)

www.rhema.org

RHEMA Bible Training Center admits students of any race, color, or ethnic origin.